Harry Pott

and the Philosopher's Stone

Novel Study Unit

Created by J.W. Crawford

Illustrated by S. Skelton

Creator's Bio

Novel Study Author

J.W. Crawford has taught Grade 6 for nearly a decade now, and has used his favourite book, *Harry Potter and the Philosopher's Stone*, as a novel study unit every year. Along with teaching, Mr. Crawford is also a published writer.

Illustrator

S. Skelton is a digital illustrator. More examples of her work can be found on her Instagram account:

https://www.instagram.com/shaeoverrated

For enquiries about her artwork, please contact Shae at:

shaeoverrated@gmail.com

This UNOFFICIAL novel study unit is designed to be used as a resource guide with the novel, *Harry Potter and the Philosopher's Stone*, written by J.K. Rowling and published by Bloomsbury Publishing Plc.

Each chapter of this novel study unit contains a Reading Comprehension piece and an activity. The comprehension is broken down into four categories. **Main Idea, Recalling Facts, Inferences,** and **Vocabulary**.

Main Idea **(3 Marks)**	In this section, students will be asked to create a paragraph that shows the main idea of the chapter. For the main idea, students should be focusing on the **big ideas** from the chapter only, not the smaller details.
Recalling Facts **(10 Marks)**	This section for each chapter contains 10 multiple choice questions based on information in the chapter.
Inferences **(10 Marks)**	In this section, students will be asked to make an inference (educated guess) about 5 questions created from the chapter. Students will need to consider the content in the chapter to answer the questions. They will need to provide evidence that supports their inference.
Vocabulary **(7 Marks)**	In this section, students will be asked to find the definition for 5 words found within the chapter. They will then need to use 2 of those words to create original sentences.

At the back of this unit, there is a section of **Doodle Notes Pages**. These pages are designed for students with busy hands! Add the doodle notes pages to the chapter questions, and have the students draw doodles of main events that occur within each chapter. This can help them remember the big ideas in the chapter!

At the end of the unit, there is also a cumulative project that teachers may wish to use or adapt to fit their needs. This assignment contains 3 elements: A Narrative Story, an Expository project, and an Artistic project.

Table of Contents

Completion Checklist
Use this checklist to keep track of your work throughout this novel study unit.

Activity	Complete
Pre-Read Activity	
Chapter 1: The Boy Who Lived	
Chapter 2: The Vanishing Glass	
Chapter 3: The Letters from No One	
Chapter 4: The Keeper of the Keys	
Chapter 5: Diagon Alley	
Chapter 6: The Journey from Platform Nine and Three-Quarters	
Chapter 7: The Sorting Hat	
Chapter 8: The Potions Master	
Chapter 9: The Midnight Duel	
Chapter 10: Hallowe'en	
Chapter 11: Quidditch	
Chapter 12: The Mirror of Erised	
Chapter 13: Nicholas Flamel	
Chapter 14: Norbert the Norwegian Ridgeback	
Chapter 15: The Forbidden Forest	
Chapter 16: Through the Trapdoor	
Chapter 17: The Man with Two Faces	
Final Project	

Pre-Read Activity

Based on the title and cover of the book, what do you think this Novel will be about?

Write a paragraph to describe what you think this book will be about. Your paragraph should be at least 4 - 5 sentences long.

```
M Z I O I M S P O H H C T I D D I U Q O W L M I R R O R T M
R S L W O T Y O W E S I U E Y U V W Y O W I Z A R D S E U P
V E D J T R A Q X W C J B N S Y V C U C X I Z R T B G F S O
B H D S A W S C D H U L E O O O Y Y M L K X E H D M I S A T
N C C R G I J P F O F R B I Y C K H E V W B P W U P W J M T
Y T B D H N H V V M L O P M U T P P C L L J F A V C D U T E
N I T N O G B Z R U J Y R R A H R F Q M L R I D D L E S S R
L W Q B S A Z J W S K S S E J I B A R A L A L P O K H N I D
E G U C T R U E F T D E Y H R N A E N O S N N S T K L O R M
H R C T S D J P A N W U W S L J P G E S N B G O P G W I H D
A N G Q B I S A U O F K M A S M E C I K F N D R G T U T C T
L M O O R U N N G T B Z B B U T K V J Z I I E E Y A A O P M
L E V R B M N S H B O A R J L C T S K T A H G N N Z I P S M
O D E C B L L Q P E E U I S T E K O L M P C R U G C X D Z Q
W F Q V F E I B I N E Z T Y T Q D E G O G N Y L R W K D F V
E T W C T V R N M A E M D E M R M O S N E S R I Y A Y B E G
E B O T A I N T S M V A E W R S A O R A I O A D F N T A H F
N H E C Z O B D H E J G U F T Z L W U E I R J H F D J I N O
K R V E R S A A W D N I N D B I L T G C O T G R I J U A O V
S M Z E Y A L Q T H P C S U H C W A A O P I E Z N B C K J N
T R A V E N C L A W A F L P R Y K W N F H N Y U D B H M L V
S Y X C S N X C E F K A V X O H K A O L C G K D O I R H F W
R Q Y R M K W A X V O L D E M O R T N K Q H E V R L O M H I
Y P A B T S S B O I C D U R S L E Y S I U A H A L A M W Y C
R X Y P N L E F G M C G O N A G A L L X M T F E O A C F Q Q
B F E D E N T O L L I V A N D E R S N E D F R R O P N O P I
P D A Y O F B Q T O G X T J O Q D M C R Z R R H A G R I D W
L Q S T T E L I O T C G V H A Z B A L S I S L Y T H E R I N
Y T S I I F L O V H R S H U F F L E P U F F Q C R W Y G D K
I N Q H N O X O U U P Y L R N I C A Q B Y L A W L H R K E E
```

Discover words from our Novel Study Unit, *Harry Potter and the Philosopher's Stone*, in the word search above! The word list is on the back of the page!

Check off each word as you find it!

☐ Christmas	☐ Hogwarts	☐ Ravenclaw
☐ Cloak	☐ Hufflepuff	☐ Riddles
☐ Curse	☐ Jumper	☐ Ron
☐ Diagon Alley	☐ Letters	☐ Slytherin
☐ Draco	☐ Library	☐ Smeltings
☐ Dumbledore	☐ Magic	☐ Snape
☐ Dursleys	☐ McGonagall	☐ Sorting Hat
☐ Ghosts	☐ Mirror	☐ Stone
☐ Goblins	☐ Norbert	☐ Toilet
☐ Gringotts	☐ Ollivanders	☐ Transfiguration
☐ Gryffindor	☐ Owls	☐ Voldemort
☐ Hagrid	☐ Philosopher	☐ Wand
☐ Halloween	☐ Potions	☐ Weasleys
☐ Harry	☐ Potter	☐ Wingardium Leviosa
☐ Hedwig	☐ Put Outer	☐ Witches
☐ Hermione	☐ Quidditch	☐ Wizards
☐ He Who Must Not Be Named	☐ Quirrell	

Owl Bookmarks: Have your students color in their own personalized owls to use as bookmarks throughout the novel study unit! Laminate them to keep them in good shape!

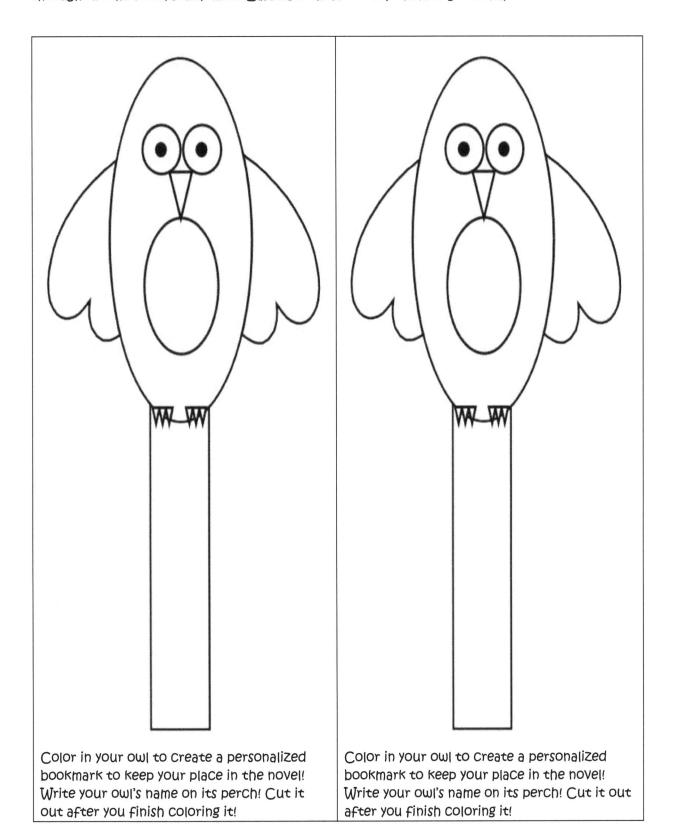

Color in your owl to create a personalized bookmark to keep your place in the novel! Write your owl's name on its perch! Cut it out after you finish coloring it!

Color in your owl to create a personalized bookmark to keep your place in the novel! Write your owl's name on its perch! Cut it out after you finish coloring it!

Chapter 1
The Boy Who Lived — Title Page

Chapter 1
The Boy Who Lived

Main Idea

In your own words, write a paragraph describing the main idea of *Chapter 1*. Use complete sentences in your answer. Remember, when describing the Main Idea of a story, you want to stick to the important pieces of information!

_____ / 3

Recalling Facts

1) What is the address of the Dursley's house?
   a. Number 14 Privet Drive
   b. Number 4 Private Road
   c. Number 4 Privet Street
   d. Number 4 Privet Drive

2) What was Vernon Dursley's occupation (job)?
   a. Director of Grunnings, a drill company
   b. Assistant Manager of Grunnings, a drill company
   c. Salesperson for Grunnings, a drill company
   d. Owner of Grunnings, a drill company

3) What is the Dursleys' greatest fear?
   a. Strange nonsense happening around them
   b. People learning about the Potters
   c. Their son's bad temper
   d. People finding out they are not normal

4) While walking to the bakery, what does Mr. Dursley hear that distresses him?
   a. Some people are talking about a boy named "Potter"
   b. Owls are flying in broad daylight
   c. There have been meteor showers
   d. Somebody had passed away

5) What strikes Mr. Dursley as strange about the man he bumps into?
   a. Nothing; the man is completely normal
   b. The man has a long beard tucked into his belt
   c. The man was wearing a violet cloak and wasn't upset
   d. The man was whispering secrets with somebody else

6) Where does Albus Dumbledore appear?
      a. On the doorstep of the Dursleys' house
      b. In the driveway of the Dursleys' house
      c. On the roof of one of the houses down the block
      d. On the corner of Privet Drive

7) What rumour did Professor McGonagall hear about Lily and James Potter?
      a. They were killed in a car crash
      b. They were killed by Voldemort
      c. They lost their son
      d. They helped Voldemort

8) Who is Dumbledore waiting for, that Professor McGonagall is unsure of?
      a. A giant named Hagrid
      b. Vernon Dursley
      c. Petunia and Dudley Dursley
      d. A wizard in a violet cloak

9) How does the writer describe Hagrid's size?
      a. An average man with dustbin lid hands
      b. As big as a car
      c. The size of a dolphin
      d. Simply too big to be allowed

10) What strange scar does Dumbledore have on his knee?
      a. A perfect map of the London Underground
      b. A perfect map of the London sewer system
      c. A perfect likeness of Hogwarts School of Witchcraft and Wizardry
      d. A perfect likeness of himself

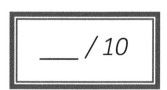

____ / 10

Inferences

An *inference* is a conclusion you can make based on the information you are given. The answer is not directly given to you.

Answer the following questions by making inferences based on information from *Harry Potter and the Philosopher's Stone*. Circle **True** if the inference is correct, or **False** if the inference is incorrect. In one or two sentences, explain your answer.

1) Vernon Dursley enjoys meeting strangers.	TRUE	FALSE
Explanation:		

2) Petunia Dursley likes to know secrets about everyone.	TRUE	FALSE
Explanation:		

3) Albus Dumbledore is a patient man.	TRUE	FALSE

Explanation:

4) Hagrid is an intimidating, angry giant.	TRUE	FALSE

Explanation:

5) The Dursleys will be a good place for Harry to grow up.	TRUE	FALSE

Explanation:

____ / 10

Vocabulary

Look up the meaning of the following words:

Mysterious	
Nonsense	
Unusual	
Persuade	
Slinking	

Create two sentences, using a different vocabulary word from the list above in each sentence.

Vocabulary Word:

Sentence:

Vocabulary Word:

Sentence:

____ / 7

Chapter 2
The Vanishing Glass — Title Page

Chapter 2
The Vanishing Glass

Main Idea

In your own words, write a paragraph describing the main idea of *Chapter 2*. Use complete sentences in your answer. Remember, when describing the Main Idea of a story, you want to stick to the important pieces of information!

___ / 3

Recalling Facts

1) What pleasant, recurring dream has Harry been experiencing?
    a. A dream about a flying motorcycle
    b. A flash of green light and a high-pitched scream
    c. Owls flying around in broad daylight
    d. Living with a different family

2) How often does Harry receive a haircut?
    a. More than all the boys in his class combined
    b. Once every couple of months
    c. Once every couple of weeks
    d. Once a year

3) Why does Dudley have a tantrum about his presents?
    a. He didn't like any of them
    b. The presents weren't expensive enough
    c. He had less presents than in previous years
    d. Harry didn't get him a present

4) What news makes Harry very happy to hear?
    a. Mrs. Figg had a chocolate cake to share
    b. Mrs. Figg had broken her leg
    c. Mrs. Figg wouldn't be able to take him for the day
    d. Dudley's friend, Piers Polkiss, was coming with them to the zoo

5) Why couldn't Harry wear Dudley's old jumper?
    a. It was too big
    b. It had a rip in one of the sleeves
    c. Dudley didn't want to share his clothes
    d. The shirt kept shrinking

6) At the zoo, what was unusual about the boa constrictor?
   a. It was impossibly large
   b. The boa constrictor originally came from Brazil
   c. The boa constrictor could understand Harry
   d. The boa constrictor was unusually small

7) What did the boa constrictor do to Dudley and Piers after the glass vanished?
   a. Tried to bite their arms
   b. Wrapped itself around them
   c. Spoke to them
   d. Snapped at their feet

8) What made Uncle Vernon angry when they were in the car after the zoo?
   a. Harry broke the glass and let the boa constrictor out
   b. Harry pushed Dudley towards the boa constrictor
   c. Piers said Harry was talking to the boa constrictor
   d. Harry laughed at how afraid Dudley had been of the boa constrictor

9) What strange vision did Harry sometimes have?
   a. A blinding flash of green light
   b. Somebody screaming his name
   c. A mysterious man with a long beard
   d. Strange people bowing to him

10) What does Harry believe happened to his parents?
   a. They moved and left him behind
   b. They were killed in a car crash
   c. They had left Harry at the Dursleys' and disappeared
   d. They were killed in a plane crash

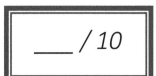

_____ / 10

Inferences

An *inference* is a conclusion you can make based on the information you are given. The answer is not directly given to you.

Answer the following questions by making inferences based on information from *Harry Potter and the Philosopher's Stone*. Circle **True** if the inference is correct, or **False** if the inference is incorrect. In one or two sentences, explain your answer.

1) Harry's dream at the beginning of the chapter has a significant meaning.	TRUE	FALSE
Explanation:		

2) Harry enjoys spending time with Mrs. Figg.	TRUE	FALSE
Explanation:		

3) The Dursleys trusted Harry to be good.	TRUE	FALSE

Explanation:

4) Uncle Vernon believed Harry had nothing to do with the boa constrictor getting free.	TRUE	FALSE

Explanation:

5) Harry was a normal boy.	TRUE	FALSE

Explanation:

_____ / 10

Vocabulary

Look up the meaning of the following words:

Mantelpiece	
Cupboard	
Tantrum	
Jumper	
Gibber	

Create two sentences, using a different vocabulary word from the list above in each sentence.

Vocabulary Word:

Sentence:

Vocabulary Word:

Sentence:

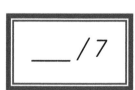

____ / 7

Chapter 3
The Letters From No One — Title Page

Name: _____

Chapter 3
The Letters From No One

Main Idea

In your own words, write a paragraph describing the main idea of *Chapter 3*. Use complete sentences in your answer. Remember, when describing the Main Idea of a story, you want to stick to the important pieces of information!

_____ / 3

Recalling Facts

1) How long was Harry punished for releasing the boa constrictor?
   a. Until summer holidays.
   b. One week.
   c. One month.
   d. Two months.

2) Why did Harry spend as much time outside as possible?
   a. He really enjoyed the warmth from the sun.
   b. When he was outside, the Dursley's couldn't punish him.
   c. It helped him avoid "Harry-hunting."
   d. The Dursley's didn't want him hanging around the house.

3) What was Aunt Petunia washing in grey water?
   a. Harry's bedroom sheets.
   b. Harry's summer clothing to make a new school uniform.
   c. The living room curtains.
   d. Dudley's old clothes to make a new school uniform.

4) What was unique about the letter meant for Harry?
   a. It had his cupboard listed on the address.
   b. It was directed to the Dursleys.
   c. It said "confidential" on the envelope.
   d. It was written on black paper.

5) How did Harry get caught when he tried to wake up early to get the mail?
   a. He fell down the stairs and woke the Dursley's.
   b. Aunt Petunia was already awake and making breakfast.
   c. Dudley heard him get up and tattled.
   d. He stepped on Uncle Vernon's face.

6) Why does Uncle Vernon like Sundays?
      a. He doesn't have to work on Sundays.
      b. There is no post on Sundays.
      c. On Sundays, the family spends time together.
      d. His favourite television show is on Sundays.

7) What made Uncle Vernon look dangerous?
      a. The veins in his head were pulsing.
      b. His face went a dark shade of purple.
      c. Half of his moustache was missing.
      d. His hair was poking out in every direction.

8) What television show was Dudley angry about missing?
      a. The Great Humberto.
      b. A game show.
      c. A show about aliens.
      d. A sports show.

9) What rations did Uncle Vernon bring for his family?
      a. Canned food and juice boxes.
      b. Tins of sardines and ketchup packets.
      c. Bananas and packets of crisps.
      d. He forgot to bring food.

10) Before there was a knock at the door, what was Harry planning on doing?
      a. Waking up Dudley to annoy him.
      b. Waking up Uncle Vernon to annoy him.
      c. Going for a walk outside the shack.
      d. Starting a fire to warm up by.

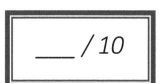

____ / 10

Inferences

An *inference* is a conclusion you can make based on the information you are given. The answer is not directly given to you.

Answer the following questions by making inferences based on information from *Harry Potter and the Philosopher's Stone*. Circle **True** if the inference is correct, or **False** if the inference is incorrect. In one or two sentences, explain your answer.

1) Dudley is reckless with his possessions.	TRUE	FALSE
Explanation:		

2) Harry was happy summer was coming to an end.	TRUE	FALSE
Explanation:		

3) Harry was happy with his new school's outfit.	TRUE	FALSE

Explanation:

4) Receiving mail was a new experience for Harry.	TRUE	FALSE

Explanation:

5) Uncle Vernon was very concerned with his family's safety.	TRUE	FALSE

Explanation:

____ / 10

Vocabulary

Look up the meaning of the following words:

Comprehensive	
Knickerbockers	
Informed	
Bawling	
Rations	

Create two sentences, using a different vocabulary word from the list above in each sentence.

Vocabulary Word: _____

Sentence:

Vocabulary Word: _____

Sentence:

___ / 7

Chapter 4
The Keeper of the Keys — Title Page

Chapter 4
The Keeper of the Keys

Main Idea

In your own words, write a paragraph describing the main idea of *Chapter 4*. Use complete sentences in your answer. Remember, when describing the Main Idea of a story, you want to stick to the important pieces of information!

_____ / 3

Recalling Facts

1) What did Uncle Vernon bring as protection against the intruder?
   - a. A rifle.
   - b. A cricket bat.
   - c. A shotgun.
   - d. A frying pan.

2) How does Hagrid describe Harry when he first talks to him?
   - a. Harry looks just like his dad.
   - b. Harry looks just like his mom.
   - c. Harry looks just like his mom, with his dad's eyes.
   - d. Harry looks just like his dad, with his mom's eyes.

3) What did Hagrid bring for Harry as a gift?
   - a. A slightly squashed pie.
   - b. A slightly squashed cake.
   - c. A picture of Harry's parents.
   - d. A letter from Harry's parents.

4) What is Hagrid's job at Hogwarts?
   - a. Caretaker of Grounds.
   - b. Keeper of Keys and Security.
   - c. Keeper of Keys and Grounds.
   - d. Caretaker of Keys and Grounds.

5) What does Harry admit that *first* shocks Hagrid?
   - a. He didn't know he was a wizard.
   - b. He has never read any of the letters he was sent.
   - c. He has never heard of Hogwarts.
   - d. He didn't know how his parents really died.

6) What was Dumbledore's relationship with Voldemort?
     a. They were old friends.
     b. Voldemort was Dumbledore's favourite student.
     c. Dumbledore was the only one Voldemort feared.
     d. They were in the same classes together.

7) What does Hagrid believe happened to Voldemort?
     a. He lost his powers and went into hiding.
     b. He was killed.
     c. He went into hiding to plan his revenge.
     d. He was replaced by another dark wizard.

8) How many years will Harry have to attend Hogwarts for?
     a. 5 years.
     b. 6 years.
     c. 7 years.
     d. 8 years.

9) What magic did Hagrid do to Dudley as punishment?
     a. He gave Dudley a pig's tail.
     b. He gave Dudley a pig's snout.
     c. He made Dudley feel very sick.
     d. He shrunk Dudley to the size of a mouse.

10) Why isn't Hagrid supposed to use magic?
     a. He isn't very well trained.
     b. He was expelled from Hogwarts.
     c. He isn't a wizard.
     d. It might alert the Muggles.

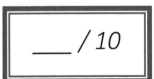

____ / 10

Inferences

An *inference* is a conclusion you can make based on the information you are given. The answer is not directly given to you.

Answer the following questions by making inferences based on information from *Harry Potter and the Philosopher's Stone*. Circle **True** if the inference is correct, or **False** if the inference is incorrect. In one or two sentences, explain your answer.

1) Hagrid is incredibly strong.	TRUE	FALSE
Explanation:		

2) Uncle Vernon is a confident and brave person.	TRUE	FALSE
Explanation:		

3) Aunt Petunia was very unhappy when she learned her sister was a witch.	TRUE	FALSE

Explanation:

_____

_____

_____

_____

4) Hagrid is very loyal to Albus Dumbledore.	TRUE	FALSE

Explanation:

_____

_____

_____

_____

5) Dumbledore trusts Hagrid with important matters.	TRUE	FALSE

Explanation:

_____

_____

_____

_____

____ / 10

Name: _____

Vocabulary

Look up the meaning of the following words:

Strode	
Bewildered	
Quill	
Scandal	
Expelled	

Create two sentences, using a different vocabulary word from the list above in each sentence.

Vocabulary Word: _____

Sentence:

Vocabulary Word: _____

Sentence:

___ / 7

Chapter 5
Diagon Alley — Title Page

Chapter 5
Diagon Alley

Main Idea

In your own words, write a paragraph describing the main idea of *Chapter 5*. Use complete sentences in your answer. Remember, when describing the Main Idea of a story, you want to stick to the important pieces of information!

_____ / 3

Recalling Facts

1) When Harry woke up the next morning, how did he feel?
   a. Excited because he was a wizard.
   b. Confused, because he didn't know what to do next.
   c. Sad, because he thought it had been a dream.
   d. Afraid, because there was a giant on the couch.

2) What was strange about the owl that Hagrid introduced to Harry?
   a. It was waiting to get paid for bringing a newspaper.
   b. It was brown with white eye rings.
   c. It was waiting quietly for some attention.
   d. It was searching Hagrid's coat for food.

3) What made Harry feel uncomfortable?
   a. He received a lot of money for his birthday.
   b. He had to ask the Dursleys for some money.
   c. He didn't want to be a wizard.
   d. He had to tell Hagrid that he had no money.

4) What is one important rule that Harry learned from the letter?
   a. First years are not allowed to have their own broomsticks.
   b. First years are allowed to choose the colour of their school robes.
   c. Animals are not allowed at Hogwarts.
   d. Students will pick up their textbooks from the library at Hogwarts.

5) What was the name of the tiny, grubby-looking pub that Hagrid brings Harry into?
   a. The Leaky Mug.
   b. The Broken Cauldron.
   c. The Leaky Cauldron.
   d. The Wizard's Brew.

6) Why does Harry feel stupid while talking to the boy in Madam Malkin's shop?
    a. The boy insults him.
    b. He realizes how little he knows about the wizarding world.
    c. He realizes he has more money than the boy.
    d. The boy insults his family and friends.

7) What happened to make Professor Quirrell so nervous all the time?
    a. He had a bad encounter with vampires and a hag.
    b. He had a bad encounter with dark wizards.
    c. He has always been a nervous wizard.
    d. He had a bad encounter with a werewolf and a witch.

8) What is Quidditch?
    a. A wizard sport, like football, but played up in the air.
    b. A type of creature that uses dark magic.
    c. A friendly creature that helps young wizards.
    d. A wizard sport, like baseball.

9) What did Ollivander find "curious?"
    a. Harry's wand had a feather from the same phoenix as Voldemort's.
    b. Harry's wand was made from the same type of wood as Voldemort's.
    c. Harry's wand was the same size as Voldemort's.
    d. Harry had the same type of wand as his father.

10) Where does Harry need to go on September 1st?
    a. Hogwarts School of Witchcraft and Wizardry.
    b. Back to the Diagon Alley.
    c. King's Cross train station.
    d. Back to Number 4 Privet Drive.

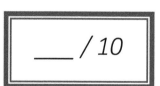

_____ / 10

Inferences

An ***inference*** is a conclusion you can make based on the information you are given. The answer is not directly given to you.

Answer the following questions by making inferences based on information from *Harry Potter and the Philosopher's Stone*. Circle **True** if the inference is correct, or **False** if the inference is incorrect. In one or two sentences, explain your answer.

1) Harry Potter is very excited about learning he is a wizard.	TRUE	FALSE
Explanation:		

2) Hagrid believes that the Ministry of Magic is doing a wonderful job.	TRUE	FALSE
Explanation:		

3) Professor Quirrell is not a very confident person.	TRUE	FALSE

Explanation:

4) Harry Potter expected that many wizards would know who he is.	TRUE	FALSE

Explanation:

5) Hagrid is very proud of his relationship with Professor Dumbledore.	TRUE	FALSE

Explanation:

___ / 10

Vocabulary

Look up the meaning of the following words:

Cauldron	
Parchment	
Awkwardly	
Flitting	
Destined	

Create two sentences, using a different vocabulary word from the list above in each sentence.

Vocabulary Word: _____

Sentence:

Vocabulary Word: _____

Sentence:

_____ / 7

Name: _____

Chapter 6

The Journey from Platform 9 and Three-Quarters — Title Page

Chapter 6
The Journey from Platform 9 and Three Quarters

Main Idea

In your own words, write a paragraph describing the main idea of *Chapter 6*. Use complete sentences in your answer. Remember, when describing the Main Idea of a story, you want to stick to the important pieces of information!

_____ / 3

Name: _____

Recalling Facts

1) What does Harry decide to name his new owl?
      a. Hedwig
      b. Headwig
      c. Snowy
      d. Bullet

2) The platform at King's Cross station that Harry has to enter is what number?
      a. Platform 10
      b. Platform 9 and a half
      c. Platform 9 and 3/4
      d. Between platforms 10 and 11

3) How does the plump woman tell Harry he can reach the platform?
      a. Tap the bricks of a wall to make an archway
      b. Go through a hidden door
      c. Cast a spell
      d. Run through the wall

4) What is it that reveals Harry's identity?
      a. The scar on his forehead
      b. His glasses
      c. His untidy black hair
      d. A tag on his luggage

5) What does Harry say that shocks Ron Weasley?
      a. The name of Voldemort
      b. He has never used magic before
      c. His favourite Quidditch team
      d. He was brought to the platform by a giant

6) Where does Harry find a picture of Albus Dumbledore?
   a. On a poster on the train
   b. On a pamphlet in the train
   c. On a chocolate frog card
   d. On the back of a box of candies

7) According to Ron, what crime occurred at Gringott's bank?
   a. Somebody attacked a goblin
   b. Somebody stole a little parcel from a vault
   c. Somebody stole gold from a vault
   d. Someone tried to rob an empty vault

8) What insult does Draco Malfoy say to Ron?
   a. He calls him ugly
   b. He claims Ron's family is poor
   c. He calls Ron a terrible wizard
   d. He calls Ron's family evil

9) What does Hermione ask to see?
   a. Harry's lightning shaped scar
   b. What textbooks they have bought
   c. A spell Ron wants to cast on Scabbers
   d. What candy they bought from the trolley

10) How do the first years arrive at Hogwarts?
    a. The train takes them directly to the castle
    b. They take a boat, a train, then follow a path
    c. They take a train, follow a path, then take a boat
    d. They take a boat directly to the castle

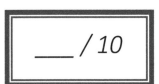

____ / 10

Inferences

An *inference* is a conclusion you can make based on the information you are given. The answer is not directly given to you.

Answer the following questions by making inferences based on information from *Harry Potter and the Philosopher's Stone*. Circle **True** if the inference is correct, or **False** if the inference is incorrect. In one or two sentences, explain your answer.

1) Uncle Vernon believe there is a train that will take Harry to Hogwarts	TRUE	FALSE
Explanation:		

2) The Weasley's have been to King's Cross station before	TRUE	FALSE
Explanation:		

3) Harry Potter is not well known by other students	TRUE	FALSE

Explanation:

4) Draco Malfoy is a mean, cruel boy	TRUE	FALSE

Explanation:

5) Neville is a forgetful boy	TRUE	FALSE

Explanation:

_____ / 10

Vocabulary

Look up the meaning of the following words:

Punctures	
Platform	
Barrier	
Gawped	
Compartment	

Create two sentences, using a different vocabulary word from the list above in each sentence.

Vocabulary Word:

Sentence:

Vocabulary Word:

Sentence:

_____ / 7

Chapter 7
The Sorting Hat — Title Page

Chapter 7
The Sorting Hat

Main Idea

In your own words, write a paragraph describing the main idea of *Chapter 7*. Use complete sentences in your answer. Remember, when describing the Main Idea of a story, you want to stick to the important pieces of information!

_____ / 3

Recalling Facts

1) What is the name of the professor that first meets the First Years?
   a. Madam Hooch
   b. Professor Sprout
   c. Professor McGonagall
   d. Professor Flitwick

2) What event happened that startled the students while they were waiting?
   a. Ghosts came through the back wall.
   b. One of the paintings started to talk to them.
   c. A painting fell off of the wall.
   d. The Bloody Baron waved a sword at the students.

3) What is special about the Great Hall?
   a. The tables in the room move around on their own.
   b. There are floating torches that light the room.
   c. The roof is bewitched to look like the outside sky.
   d. Fireworks erupt as the students enter.

4) What was the name of the textbook Hermione had read to find information about the school?
   a. *History of Hogwarts.*
   b. *Fantastic Beasts and Where to Find Them.*
   c. *Great Castles of Witchcraft and Wizardry.*
   d. *Hogwarts: A History*

5) What trait does the Sorting Hat say Gryffindor students possess?
   a. *Dwell the brave of heart.*
   b. *Unafraid of toil.*
   c. *Have a ready mind.*
   d. *Use any means to achieve their ends*

6) What horrible thought struck Harry as he waited his turn for the Sorting Hat?
   a. He might not be chosen for any house group.
   b. He might be chosen for Hufflepuff.
   c. He might be chosen for Ravenclaw.
   d. He might be chosen for Slytherin.

7) What ghost introduces himself to Harry and his friends?
   a. Headless Nick.
   b. Nearly Headless Nicholas.
   c. Sir Nicholas de Mimsy Porpington.
   d. Sir Nicholas de Porpington.

8) Why are students not allowed in the third-floor corridor?
   a. The corridor belongs to the ghosts.
   b. They may suffer a painful death.
   c. The professor's staff room is on the third-floor corridor.
   d. There is an evil spell on the third-floor corridor.

9) What is the name of the mischievous ghost of Hogwarts?
   a. Peeves the Poltergeist.
   b. The Bloody Baron.
   c. The Fat Friar.
   d. Peeves the ghost.

10) How do students get inside their dormitory?
    a. Ask permission from a painting.
    b. Give a password to the house prefect.
    c. Give a password to a painting.
    d. Answer a riddle.

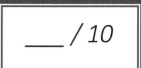

___ / 10

Inferences

An ***inference*** is a conclusion you can make based on the information you are given. The answer is not directly given to you.

Answer the following questions by making inferences based on information from *Harry Potter and the Philosopher's Stone*. Circle **True** if the inference is correct, or **False** if the inference is incorrect. In one or two sentences, explain your answer.

1) Professor McGonagall has a good sense of humour.	TRUE	FALSE
Explanation:		

2) The first-year students knew that ghosts lived in Hogwarts.	TRUE	FALSE
Explanation:		

3) Students do not get to help choose their house group.	TRUE	FALSE

Explanation:

_____

_____

_____

_____

4) Professor Dumbledore is a fan of music.	TRUE	FALSE

Explanation:

_____

_____

_____

_____

5) Peeves the Poltergeist enjoys playing tricks on new students.	TRUE	FALSE

Explanation:

_____

_____

_____

_____

_____ / 10

Vocabulary

Look up the meaning of the following words:

Magnificent	
Transparent	
Bewitched	
Airily	
Dormitory	

Create two sentences, using a different vocabulary word from the list above in each sentence.

Vocabulary Word:

Sentence:

Vocabulary Word:

Sentence:

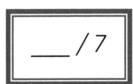

_____ / 7

Chapter 8
The Potions Master — Title Page

Chapter 8
The Potions Master

Main Idea

In your own words, write a paragraph describing the main idea of *Chapter 8*. Use complete sentences in your answer. Remember, when describing the Main Idea of a story, you want to stick to the important pieces of information!

_____ / 3

Recalling Facts

1) What is unique about the staircases at Hogwarts?
   a. There are more staircases than can be counted.
   b. The staircases move around.
   c. The staircases are impossibly long.
   d. The staircases move students like escalators.

2) What was strange about the paintings around Hogwarts?
   a. The people in the portraits played tricks on the students.
   b. The people in the portraits were actually ghosts.
   c. The people in the portraits frightened the students.
   d. The people in the portraits kept going to visit each other.

3) Which ghost was particularly helpful?
   a. Nearly Headless Nick.
   b. The Bloody Baron.
   c. Peeves the Poltergeist.
   d. The Fat Friar.

4) What happened to Professor Binns?
   a. He died in front of a fire and became a ghost.
   b. He died when a spell in class went wrong and became a ghost.
   c. He was killed by Voldemort.
   d. He was expelled for practicing Dark Magic.

5) What was Professor Quirrell's classroom like?
   a. It was full of interested magical artifacts.
   b. It smelled like garlic to ward of vampires.
   c. It was very bright because he was afraid of the dark.
   d. It was in the dungeons.

6) How did Quirrell supposedly get his turban?
    a. He took it from a vampire he defeated.
    b. It was a gift for fighting off a troublesome zombie.
    c. He made it to help ward off vampires.
    d. He won it in a wizard's duel.

7) What came as a relief to Harry?
    a. He wasn't miles behind everyone else at Hogwarts.
    b. He was sharing a potions class with Slytherin.
    c. He was well known around Hogwarts.
    d. Professor Snape doesn't teach Defense Against the Dark Arts.

8) What book does Harry think could have helped him answer Snape's questions?
    a. *One Thousand Magical Herbs and Fungi*.
    b. *Fantastic Beasts and Where to Find Them*.
    c. *Hogwarts: A History*.
    d. *Amazing Uses of Magical Herbs and Fungi*.

9) What happens when you combine root of asphodel and wormwood?
    a. It will create a chemical explosion.
    b. It creates a potion that stoppers death.
    c. It creates a powerful sleeping potion.
    d. It creates a potion that makes the drinker invisible.

10) When did the break in at Gringotts happen?
    a. On the first day of school.
    b. On Harry's birthday.
    c. The day after Harry's visit to Diagon Alley.
    d. Before Hagrid and Harry visited the bank.

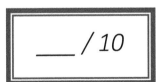

_____ / 10

Inferences

An ***inference*** is a conclusion you can make based on the information you are given. The answer is not directly given to you.

Answer the following questions by making inferences based on information from *Harry Potter and the Philosopher's Stone*. Circle **True** if the inference is correct, or **False** if the inference is incorrect. In one or two sentences, explain your answer.

1) The students of Hogwarts are very interested in Harry Potter.	TRUE	FALSE
Explanation:		

2) Argus Filch, the caretaker, enjoys the students at Hogwarts.	TRUE	FALSE
Explanation:		

3) Defence Against the Dark Arts was a very popular class.	TRUE	FALSE

Explanation:

_____
_____
_____
_____

4) Hermione Granger is a very good student.	TRUE	FALSE

Explanation:

_____
_____
_____
_____

5) Hagrid knows something about the Gringotts break-in.	TRUE	FALSE

Explanation:

_____
_____
_____
_____

_____ / 10

Vocabulary

Look up the meaning of the following words:

Queuing	
Subtle	
Register	
Investigations	
Grubby	

Create two sentences, using a different vocabulary word from the list above in each sentence.

Vocabulary Word:

Sentence:

Vocabulary Word:

Sentence:

____ / 7

Chapter 9
The Midnight Duel — Title Page

Chapter 9
The Midnight Duel

Main Idea

In your own words, write a paragraph describing the main idea of *Chapter 9*. Use complete sentences in your answer. Remember, when describing the Main Idea of a story, you want to stick to the important pieces of information!

_____ / 3

Recalling Facts

1) What surprised Harry about his thoughts towards Draco Malfoy?
   a. He hated Draco more than Dudley.
   b. Draco was actually friendly.
   c. Draco was the most hated boy at Hogwarts.
   d. He was still easier to like than Dudley.

2) What worried Harry about his first flying lesson?
   a. He didn't want to fall off and get hurt.
   b. He thought his broom wouldn't work.
   c. He worried he would be the slowest on his broom.
   d. He didn't want to look foolish in front of Malfoy.

3) What did Ron tell everyone about his flying adventures?
   a. He had once beaten his older brother Charlie in a race.
   b. He had once almost hit a hang-glider.
   c. He had once flown through a flock of owls.
   d. He had fallen twenty feet from his broom once.

4) What is a Remembrall?
   a. An item that helps tell when somebody is angry.
   b. A wizard toy used to help teach how to fly.
   c. An item that helps remind people if they forget something.
   d. One of the balls used in a Quidditch match.

5) What happened to Neville on his first attempt at flying?
   a. He lost control of his broom and was injured.
   b. He crashed into another student and both were hurt.
   c. He dropped his Remembrall and lost it.
   d. He turned out to be quite good on a broom.

6) What curse did Ron threaten to use on Hermione and Neville?
     a. The Curse of the Bogies.
     b. The Curse of Vomiting.
     c. The Curse of the Runny Nose.
     d. The Curse of Stinky Feet.

7) What wrong move did Ron make with Peeves?
     a. He threw something at him.
     b. He threatened the poltergeist.
     c. He called him a nasty name.
     d. He tried to hit him.

8) How did Harry, Hermione and Ron escape Argus Filch and Mrs. Norris?
     a. They hid in a locked room.
     b. They use a spell to make themselves invisible.
     c. The hid behind a giant suit of armour.
     d. They told Peeves to make a distraction.

9) Who caught the children as they escaped from the giant dog?
     a. The Fat Lady that guards the entrance to their dormitory.
     b. Percy the Prefect.
     c. Professor Snape.
     d. Nearly Headless Nick.

10) What did Hermione suggest that shocked Ron?
     a. She was going to tell Professor McGonagall what happened.
     b. She was excited about their accidental adventure.
     c. The dog was guarding a secret doorway.
     d. Getting expelled would be worse than getting killed.

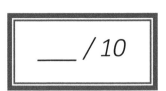

___ / 10

Name: _____

Inferences

An *inference* is a conclusion you can make based on the information you are given. The answer is not directly given to you.

Answer the following questions by making inferences based on information from *Harry Potter and the Philosopher's Stone*. Circle **True** if the inference is correct, or **False** if the inference is incorrect. In one or two sentences, explain your answer.

1) Draco Malfoy is a confident flyer.	TRUE	FALSE
Explanation:		

2) Dean Thomas comes from a Muggle family.	TRUE	FALSE
Explanation:		

3) The Remembrall didn't help Neville with his memory problems.	TRUE	FALSE

Explanation:

4) Harry Potter has a natural talent for flying.	TRUE	FALSE

Explanation:

5) Peeves helps Filch catch students who are breaking rules.	TRUE	FALSE

Explanation:

_____ / 10

Vocabulary

Look up the meaning of the following words:

Reasonably	
Boastful	
Gloatingly	
Quaver	
Puzzlement	

Create two sentences, using a different vocabulary word from the list above in each sentence.

Vocabulary Word: _____

Sentence:

Vocabulary Word: _____

Sentence:

____ / 7

Chapter 10

Hallowe'en — Title Page

Chapter 10

Hallowe'en

Main Idea

In your own words, write a paragraph describing the main idea of *Chapter 10*. Use complete sentences in your answer. Remember, when describing the Main Idea of a story, you want to stick to the important pieces of information!

_____ / 3

Recalling Facts

1) What do the owls drop in front of Harry during breakfast?
      a. The Daily Prophet newspaper.
      b. A new broomstick.
      c. A Halloween costume.
      d. A note from Professor McGonagall.

2) What are the positions on a Quidditch team?
      a. Goaltender, forwards, defence
      b. Keeper, Defence, Seeker, Beaters
      c. Keeper, Beaters, Chasers, Seeker
      d. Keeper, Bludgers, Chasers, Seeker

3) How does a Quidditch game end?
      a. When the Seeker catches the Golden Bludger.
      b. When a Chaser catches the Golden Snitch.
      c. When a team scores 150 points.
      d. When the Seeker catches the Golden Snitch.

4) Why does Professor Flitwick applaud Hermione in Charms class?
      a. She successfully uses a levitation spell.
      b. She successfully uses a door opening spell.
      c. She successfully creates a proper potion to cure boils.
      d. She received 100% on an assignment.

5) Why is Hermione upset after charms class?
      a. She lost points for Gryffindor.
      b. The Slytherin students made fun of her.
      c. She overhears Ron and Harry talking about her.
      d. She got in trouble from Professor Flitwick.

6) What teacher warns the school about the troll?
   a. Professor Flitwick.
   b. Professor McGonagall.
   c. Professor Dumbledore.
   d. Professor Quirrell.

7) What instructions does Dumbledore give the students?
   a. Return to their house dormitories with their prefects.
   b. Remain in the Great Hall with the doors locked.
   c. Return to their house dormitories with a teacher.
   d. Go to the nearest dormitory and lock themselves inside.

8) What did Harry and Ron do that was a big mistake?
   a. Chased the troll into the boys' bathroom.
   b. Locked the troll into the girls' bathroom while Hermione was inside.
   c. Teased the troll in the hallways and made it angry.
   d. Locked the troll in the third-floor corridor with the three headed dog.

9) How does Ron end the battle with the troll?
   a. He uses *wingardium leviosa* to drop the troll's own club on its head.
   b. He knocks the troll out with a large stone.
   c. He climbs onto the troll and sticks his wand up its nose.
   d. He trips the troll and sends it sprawling to the floor.

10) What lie does Hermione say about the troll encounter?
   a. She told Professor Quirrell to warn the other teachers.
   b. She defeated the troll with the *wingardium leviosa* spell.
   c. She thought she could stop it, and Ron and Harry saved her.
   d. Ron and Harry let the troll inside.

___ / 10

Name: _____

Inferences

An *inference* is a conclusion you can make based on the information you are given. The answer is not directly given to you.

Answer the following questions by making inferences based on information from *Harry Potter and the Philosopher's Stone*. Circle **True** if the inference is correct, or **False** if the inference is incorrect. In one or two sentences, explain your answer.

1) Hermione thinks it's great that Harry received a present at breakfast.	TRUE	FALSE
Explanation:		

2) The Keeper is the most important position in Quidditch.	TRUE	FALSE
Explanation:		

3) Hermione Granger has a difficult time making friends	TRUE	FALSE
Explanation:		

4) Mountain Trolls are difficult creatures to defeat.	TRUE	FALSE
Explanation:		

5) Ron and Harry think Hermione would make a loyal friend.	TRUE	FALSE
Explanation:		

____ / 10

Vocabulary

Look up the meaning of the following words:

Keen	
Fluttered	
Recited	
Substitutes	
Trousers	

Create two sentences, using a different vocabulary word from the list above in each sentence.

Vocabulary Word:

Sentence:

Vocabulary Word:

Sentence:

_____ / 7

Chapter 11
Quidditch — Title Page

Chapter 11
Quidditch

Main Idea

In your own words, write a paragraph describing the main idea of *Chapter 11*. Use complete sentences in your answer. Remember, when describing the Main Idea of a story, you want to stick to the important pieces of information!

_____ / 3

Recalling Facts

1) What exciting event happens in November?
    a. The students have their first exams.
    b. The Quidditch season begins.
    c. There is a ghost parade through the school.
    d. The students learn how to use defensive magic.

2) What happens if Gryffindor beats Slytherin in their Quidditch match?
    a. It will be their first ever victory against Slytherin.
    b. They will be in first place in the House Cup standings.
    c. They will win the House Cup.
    d. They will move into second place in the House Cup standings.

3) What book is Harry hoping to get back from Professor Snape?
    a. *Fantastic Beasts and Where to Find Them.*
    b. *Hogwarts: A History.*
    c. *Quidditch Through the Ages.*
    d. *The Monster Book of Monsters.*

4) What did Harry see in the staff room when he opened the door?
    a. Professor Snape was helping Filch bandage his leg.
    b. Caretaker Filch was helping Snape bandage his leg.
    c. The teachers were arguing over who let the troll in on Halloween.
    d. The staff room was completely empty.

5) What does Harry think Professor Snape was responsible for?
    a. The break-in at Gringott's Bank.
    b. Putting the three-headed dog in the third floor corridor.
    c. Setting the troll loose in Hogwarts.
    d. Slytherin being ahead of Gryffindor in House Points.

6) How did some of the Gryffindor Quidditch team fans surprise Harry?
   a. They each carried signs that said *Potter for President*.
   b. They made a giant Gryffindor banner to cheer on the team.
   c. They were so loud that they drowned out the Slytherin fans.
   d. They made a giant *Potter for President* banner to cheer Harry on.

7) What was Oliver Wood's game plan for Harry during the Quidditch match?
   a. He wanted Harry to stay close to the beaters so he wouldn't get hit.
   b. He wanted Harry to stay out of the way until he saw the Snitch.
   c. He wanted Harry to fly through the match until he found the Snitch.
   d. He wanted Harry to stay close to him to avoid the bludgers.

8) Why did Hagrid think Harry's broom wasn't broken when Harry lost control?
   a. Nothing but dark magic could interfere with a broom.
   b. Harry's broom was brand new, and had never been used.
   c. Harry's broom had been inspected before the match.
   d. Harry wasn't a very good flier, and it was his own fault.

9) How did Hermione help Harry regain control over his broom?
   a. She interrupted Snape by pretending to have questions about potions.
   b. She lit the bench beside Professor Snape on fire as a distraction.
   c. She yelled at Professor Snape and accused him of cheating.
   d. She lit Professor Snape's robes on fire to distract him.

10) What did Harry, Ron and Hermione learn about the three-headed dog?
    a. The dog belonged to Dumbledore and was named *Fluffy*.
    b. The dog had attacked Professor Snape when he tried to get past it.
    c. The dog belonged to Hagrid and was named *Fluffy*.
    d. The dog was actually created by a spell.

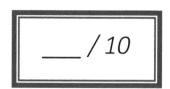

_____ / 10

Inferences

An *inference* is a conclusion you can make based on the information you are given. The answer is not directly given to you.

Answer the following questions by making inferences based on information from *Harry Potter and the Philosopher's Stone*. Circle **True** if the inference is correct, or **False** if the inference is incorrect. In one or two sentences, explain your answer.

1) Students at Hogwarts are good at keeping secrets.	TRUE	FALSE

Explanation:

2) Harry was not very confident about how he would do in his first Quidditch match.	TRUE	FALSE

Explanation:

3) Lee Jordan was heavily biased against the Slytherin Quidditch team.	TRUE	FALSE
Explanation:		

4) Hermione was afraid to break the rules at Hogwarts, even to help a friend.	TRUE	FALSE
Explanation:		

5) Hagrid believes that Snape was trying to steal something very important.	TRUE	FALSE
Explanation:		

_____ / 10

Vocabulary

Look up the meaning of the following words:

Foul	
Restless	
Chatter	
Revolting	
Jinx	

Create two sentences, using a different vocabulary word from the list above in each sentence.

Vocabulary Word:

Sentence:

Vocabulary Word:

Sentence:

___/7

Chapter 12
The Mirror of Erised — Title Page

Chapter 12
The Mirror of Erised

Main Idea

In your own words, write a paragraph describing the main idea of *Chapter 12*. Use complete sentences in your answer. Remember, when describing the Main Idea of a story, you want to stick to the important pieces of information!

___ / 3

Recalling Facts

1) Why is the dungeon an uncomfortable place for students in this chapter?
    a. It's December, and the dungeons are cold.
    b. Professor Snape runs the potions lessons.
    c. It's the favourite hang out for Slytherins.
    d. The cauldrons are too hot.

2) Why was Ron staying at Hogwarts for the holidays?
    a. He was given a long detention from Professor Snape.
    b. His family was spending their holiday with Ron at Hogwarts.
    c. His parents were visiting his brother in Romania.
    d. His parents were mad at him.

3) Why did Professor Snape take points from Gryffindor?
    a. Harry failed in a potions assignment.
    b. Ron tried to start a fight with Malfoy.
    c. Ron insulted Malfoy's family.
    d. Malfoy told Snape a lie.

4) Where does Hermione think they should be during their time before lunch?
    a. In the Great Hall studying.
    b. In their dormitory studying.
    c. In the library looking for information.
    d. In the Great Hall saving seats for lunch.

5) Which book did Harry, Ron and Hermione *not* look for information in?
    a. *Great Wizards of the Twentieth Century*.
    b. *Notable Magical Names of Our Time*.
    c. *Hogwarts: A History*.
    d. *Important Modern Magical Discoveries*.

6) Why couldn't Harry, Ron and Hermione visit the Restricted Section of the library?
   a. First years aren't smart enough for the books in the Restricted Section.
   b. Only professors are allowed in the Restricted Section.
   c. First years aren't allowed in the Restricted Section.
   d. They need a special signed note from a teacher.

7) What special gift did Harry receive from an anonymous person?
   a. A new broomstick for Quidditch.
   b. A special holiday pack of Bertie Bott's Every Flavour Beans.
   c. A jumper that would turn him invisible.
   d. A cloak that would turn him invisible.

8) Why did Professor Snape want to talk to Argus Filch?
   a. He wants to know if anyone was wandering around at night.
   b. He needs to Filch help him with a new bandage for his leg.
   c. He wants to know if anyone has been in the Restricted Section.
   d. He needs help cleaning a mess in the dungeons.

9) What did Harry see when he looked at his reflection in the Mirror of Erised?
   a. Voldemort standing behind him.
   b. His parents.
   c. Professor Dumbledore waving to him.
   d. Himself, Ron and Hermione escaping from Fluffy.

10) According to Dumbledore, what does the Mirror of Erised show?
   a. The deepest desire of our hearts.
   b. Visions from the past.
   c. Visions from the future.
   d. What someone will look like when they're older.

___ / 10

Inferences

An ***inference*** is a conclusion you can make based on the information you are given. The answer is not directly given to you.

Answer the following questions by making inferences based on information from *Harry Potter and the Philosopher's Stone*. Circle **True** if the inference is correct, or **False** if the inference is incorrect. In one or two sentences, explain your answer.

1) Harry is not excited to stay at Hogwarts for the holidays.	TRUE	FALSE
Explanation:		

2) Hagrid knows more about Nicolas Flamel than he is admitting.	TRUE	FALSE
Explanation:		

3) Madam Pince does not like first years visiting the Restricted Section of the library.	TRUE	FALSE

Explanation:

_____

_____

_____

_____

4) Hermione's parents would know something about Nicolas Flamel.	TRUE	FALSE

Explanation:

_____

_____

_____

_____

_____

5) Harry felt a connection with his father because of the Invisibility Cloak.	TRUE	FALSE

Explanation:

_____

_____

_____

_____

_____

_____ / 10

Vocabulary

Look up the meaning of the following words:

Bucking	
Blossoming	
Restricted	
Feeble	
Luminous	

Create two sentences, using a different vocabulary word from the list above in each sentence.

Vocabulary Word: _____

Sentence:

Vocabulary Word: _____

Sentence:

_____ / 7

Chapter 13
Nicolas Flamel — Title Page

Chapter 13
Nicolas Flamel

Main Idea

In your own words, write a paragraph describing the main idea of *Chapter 13*. Use complete sentences in your answer. Remember, when describing the Main Idea of a story, you want to stick to the important pieces of information!

___ / 3

Recalling Facts

1) What did Professor Dumbledore convince Harry to do?
   a. To keep his knowledge of the Mirror of Erised a secret.
   b. To learn what he could about his family through the Mirror of Erised.
   c. To not go looking for the Mirror of Erised once it was moved.
   d. That the Mirror of Erised lied about his family.

2) What bad news did Oliver Wood give the Gryffindor Quidditch team?
   a. Professor Snape would be the referee in their next game.
   b. Their next game was canceled due to poor weather.
   c. Harry wouldn't be able to play as Seeker.
   d. Professor McGonagall would be the referee in their next game.

3) What did Harry and Ron think might be good for Hermione?
   a. Breaking the rules once in awhile.
   b. Failing an assignment at school.
   c. Learning to play Wizard's Chess.
   d. Losing at Wizard's Chess.

4) What unfortunate thing happened to Neville?
   a. His nose was bleeding from a scuffle with Draco Malfoy.
   b. His legs were stuck together from a Leg-Locker Curse.
   c. He was locked out of the Gryffindor common room…again.
   d. He had lost Trevor the toad again.

5) What did Malfoy tell Neville that made him unhappy?
   a. He would have been better in Slytherin.
   b. He wasn't brave enough to be in Gryffindor.
   c. He would never be an adequate wizard.
   d. He was going to beat him up later.

6) Where did Harry finally discover information about Nicolas Flamel?
    a. On a Nicolas Flamel wizard card from a chocolate frog.
    b. On a Professor Dumbledore wizard card from a chocolate frog.
    c. In a book hidden in the Restricted Section of the library.
    d. From Hagrid, who accidently gave away a secret about Flamel.

7) What important information did Hermione read about Nicolas Flamel?
    a. He was the first wizard to learn how to use the Philosopher's Stone.
    b. He was the wizard who found the first Philosopher's Stone.
    c. He helped Dumbledore create the Philosopher's Stone.
    d. He was the only known maker of the Philosopher's Stone.

8) What two things does the Philosopher's Stone do?
    a. Turns metal into gold and grants the owner immortality.
    b. Turns metal into silver and grants the owner immortality.
    c. Turns metal into gold and grants the owner long life.
    d. Turns wood into gold and grants the owner immortality.

9) How did the Quidditch match end?
    a. The game was called off because of a bad accident to a player.
    b. Harry had caught the Golden Snitch, and Gryffindor won.
    c. Harry caught the Golden Snitch, but Gryffindor still lost.
    d. Gryffindor lost on a penalty shot awarded by Professor Snape.

10) What happened to Malfoy at the end of the Quidditch match?
    a. Ron gave him a black eye in a fist fight.
    b. Neville gave him a bloody nose in a fist fight.
    c. He was knocked out by a curse from Ron.
    d. He was accidentally knocked out by Crabbe and Goyle.

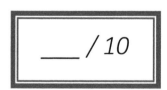

___ / 10

Inferences

An *inference* is a conclusion you can make based on the information you are given. The answer is not directly given to you.

Answer the following questions by making inferences based on information from *Harry Potter and the Philosopher's Stone*. Circle **True** if the inference is correct, or **False** if the inference is incorrect. In one or two sentences, explain your answer.

1) Professor Snape was a good choice to referee a Quidditch match.	TRUE	FALSE
Explanation:		

2) Losing at chess was good for Hermione.	TRUE	FALSE
Explanation:		

3) Today's Quidditch game will not be dangerous.	TRUE	FALSE

Explanation:

4) Ron finally had enough of Malfoy's teasing.	TRUE	FALSE

Explanation:

5) Professor Quirrell would be a bad choice to help protect the Philosopher's Stone.	TRUE	FALSE

Explanation:

___ / 10

Vocabulary

Look up the meaning of the following words:

Roaming	
Curse	
Alchemy	
Steadied	
Alarm	

Create two sentences, using a different vocabulary word from the list above in each sentence.

Vocabulary Word: _____

Sentence:

Vocabulary Word: _____

Sentence:

____ / 7

Chapter 14

Norbert the Norwegian Ridgeback — Title Page

Chapter 14
Norbert the Norwegian Ridgeback

Main Idea

In your own words, write a paragraph describing the main idea of *Chapter 14*. Use complete sentences in your answer. Remember, when describing the Main Idea of a story, you want to stick to the important pieces of information!

_____ / 3

Recalling Facts

1) What surprised Harry about Quirrell?
   a. He was actually a very good teacher.
   b. He was just pretending to be afraid.
   c. He surrendered to Snape very quickly.
   d. He was braver than Harry thought.

2) Why was the Easter holiday not as fun as the Christmas one?
   a. The teachers piled homework on the students.
   b. Too many students stayed at Hogwarts for the holiday.
   c. Wizard's Chess was no longer allowed at Hogwarts.
   d. There were no presents during the Easter holiday.

3) What types of books was Hagrid looking at in the library?
   a. He was looking up information on fire-breathing slugs.
   b. He was looking up information about unicorns.
   c. He was looking up information about dragons.
   d. He was looking through the Restricted Section for Nicholas Flamel.

4) Which professor did *not* put a protective enchantment on the Philosopher's Stone?
   a. Professor Quirrell.
   b. Professor Dumbledore.
   c. Professor Binns.
   d. Professor Snape.

5) Where did Hagrid acquire the dragon egg?
   a. From a friend in the village.
   b. From Ron's brother, Charlie, in Romania.
   c. He found it in the Forbidden Forest.
   d. He won it in a game of cards.

6) What type of dragon is Hagrid trying to hatch?
   a. Swedish Short-Snout.
   b. Norwegian Ridgeback.
   c. Hebridean Black.
   d. Hungarian Horntail.

7) What made them nervous about the dragon?
   a. Malfoy saw the dragon through the window.
   b. Norbert lit the roof of Hagrid's hut on fire.
   c. Dumbledore discovered that Hagrid had a dragon.
   d. The dragon escaped into the Forbidden Forest.

8) How did they decide to deal with Norbert to keep Hagrid from getting in trouble?
   a. Hagrid would release him into the wild.
   b. Hagrid would sell the dragon to Newt Scamander.
   c. They would send the dragon to Ron's brother, Charlie.
   d. Hagrid would give the dragon to Dumbledore to deal with.

9) What punishment did Malfoy get for sneaking out after curfew?
   a. He lost ten points for Slytherin.
   b. He lost ten points for Slytherin and received detention.
   c. He lost twenty points for Slytherin.
   d. He lost twenty points for Slytherin and received detention.

10) Why was Filch able to catch them coming down from the tower?
   a. Mrs. Norris saw them and alerted the caretaker.
   b. They had forgotten the invisibility cloak on the tower.
   c. Malfoy saw them and tattled to Filch.
   d. Peeves caught them and alerted the caretaker.

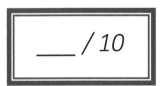

_____ / 10

Inferences

An ***inference*** is a conclusion you can make based on the information you are given. The answer is not directly given to you.

Answer the following questions by making inferences based on information from *Harry Potter and the Philosopher's Stone*. Circle **True** if the inference is correct, or **False** if the inference is incorrect. In one or two sentences, explain your answer.

1) Ron tried to encourage and support Professor Quirrell.	TRUE	FALSE
Explanation:		

2) Hagrid thinks Harry, Ron and Hermione are up to no good.	TRUE	FALSE
Explanation:		

3) It's a good thing for Muggles to know that there are dragons in the world.	TRUE	FALSE
Explanation:		

4) Dragons are a normal pet for wizards to have in the Wizarding World.	TRUE	FALSE
Explanation:		

5) Professor McGonagall was not prepared to be wandering Hogwarts at night.	TRUE	FALSE
Explanation:		

_____ / 10

Vocabulary

Look up the meaning of the following words:

Revision	
Longingly	
Philosopher	
Flattering	
Handkerchief	

Create two sentences, using a different vocabulary word from the list above in each sentence.

Vocabulary Word: _____

Sentence:

Vocabulary Word: _____

Sentence:

____ / 7

Chapter 15

The Forbidden Forest — Title Page

Chapter 15
The Forbidden Forest

Main Idea

In your own words, write a paragraph describing the main idea of *Chapter 15*. Use complete sentences in your answer. Remember, when describing the Main Idea of a story, you want to stick to the important pieces of information!

_____ / 3

Recalling Facts

1) Where did Filch take the students after they were caught out of bed?
   a. Hagrid's hut outside of the castle.
   b. Professor Snape's classroom in the dungeon.
   c. Professor Dumbledore's office.
   d. Professor McGonagall's first floor study.

2) Who did Professor McGonagall have with her when she confronted the students?
   a. Neville Longbottom.
   b. Draco Malfoy.
   c. Professor Dumbledore.
   d. Professor Snape.

3) What did Professor McGonagall think was going on?
   a. They were hiding a dragon.
   b. They lied to Malfoy to get him in trouble.
   c. They were trying to learn about the Philosopher's Stone.
   d. They were trying to find Nicholas Flamel.

4) How many points did Professor McGonagall take from Gryffindor?
   a. One hundred points.
   b. Fifty points.
   c. One hundred fifty points.
   d. Two hundred points.

5) What did Harry offer to do for the Gryffindor Quidditch team?
   a. To play even harder.
   b. To pay for new Quidditch equipment.
   c. To put in extra practice time.
   d. To resign from the team.

6) What did Harry overhear from a classroom?
     a. Professor Quirrell being threatened.
     b. Professor Quirrell arguing with Professor Snape.
     c. Peeves the Poltergeist causing trouble.
     d. Caretaker Filch laughing about him getting into trouble.

7) What did Harry think was the best thing to do about new information he discovered about the Philosopher's Stone?
     a. Go and tell Dumbledore.
     b. Go and tell Professor McGonagall.
     c. Go and uncover the truth about the Philosopher's Stone.
     d. Go and find more information from the library.

8) What type of creatures does Malfoy believe lives in the Forbidden Forest?
     a. Unicorns.
     b. Dragons.
     c. Werewolves.
     d. Centaurs.

9) Why would the hooded figure be drinking unicorn blood?
     a. He is using it to stay alive.
     b. He is drinking it to gain powers.
     c. He is using it to help create dark magic.
     d. He is a creature that lives on the blood of other animals.

10) What did Harry find when he returned to his room?
     a. A note from Hagrid asking to see him.
     b. A note along with his returned invisibility cloak.
     c. A message from Oliver Wood, captain of his Quidditch team.
     d. A message from Dumbledore asking for his help.

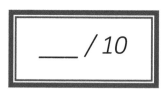

____ / 10

Inferences

An *inference* is a conclusion you can make based on the information you are given. The answer is not directly given to you.

Answer the following questions by making inferences based on information from *Harry Potter and the Philosopher's Stone*. Circle **True** if the inference is correct, or **False** if the inference is incorrect. In one or two sentences, explain your answer.

1) Neville understood that Harry and the others weren't trying to play a trick on him.	TRUE	FALSE
Explanation:		

2) The Gryffindor Quidditch team was very unhappy that Harry had lost them house points.	TRUE	FALSE
Explanation:		

3) Draco Malfoy was NOT afraid to go into the Forbidden Forest.	TRUE	FALSE

Explanation:

4) Centaurs believe there are messages in the night sky.	TRUE	FALSE

Explanation:

5) Voldemort is the most powerful wizard in history.	TRUE	FALSE

Explanation:

___ / 10

Vocabulary

Look up the meaning of the following words:

Astronomy	
Ashamed	
Rebellion	
Towering	
Undergrowth	

Create two sentences, using a different vocabulary word from the list above in each sentence.

Vocabulary Word:

Sentence:

Vocabulary Word:

Sentence:

___ / 7

Chapter 16
Through the Trapdoor — Title Page

Chapter 16
Through the Trapdoor

Main Idea

In your own words, write a paragraph describing the main idea of *Chapter 16*. Use complete sentences in your answer. Remember, when describing the Main Idea of a story, you want to stick to the important pieces of information!

___ / 3

Recalling Facts

1) What test-taking tool were the students given?
   a. Anti-cheating quills.
   b. Anti-cheating ink.
   c. Noise reducing ear muffs.
   d. Memory parchment.

2) What did Professor Flitwick want the students to do?
   a. Make a pineapple tap dance across a desk.
   b. Make a watermelon roll across the floor.
   c. Make a feather levitate.
   d. Turn a mouse into a snuff-box.

3) Harry's old nightmare returned, with a new terrible vision:
   a. Voldemort casting a spell towards him.
   b. Fluffy preparing to eat him.
   c. A hooded figure dripping blood.
   d. A dead unicorn.

4) Why did Hermione tell Harry to go and visit Madame Pomfrey?
   a. He felt sick from all the exams.
   b. His scar was hurting badly.
   c. To ask about Snape's injured leg.
   d. He fell off his broom in Quidditch.

5) In order to calm down Fluffy, a person would need to:
   a. Find a way to exercise him immensely.
   b. Give him a large meal.
   c. Use a sleep spell on him.
   d. Play him some music and send him to sleep.

6) Why couldn't Harry tell Dumbledore about what he discovered?
   a. Dumbledore was called out by the Ministry of Magic.
   b. Someone sent a fake note to lure him away.
   c. Professor McGonagall didn't believe Harry.
   d. Professor Dumbledore wasn't interested in hearing Harry's news.

7) How did they suggest they could keep an eye on Snape?
   a. They could cast a tracking spell on him.
   b. Hermione could wait for him outside of the staff room.
   c. They could use Harry's invisibility cloak.
   d. Ron could put Scabbers in Snape's cloak pocket.

8) Why does Harry think it's worth getting expelled to stop Snape?
   a. Snape wants to bring Voldemort back.
   b. They could get Snape fired.
   c. They don't want Professor Quirrell to get hurt.
   d. It might help their damaged reputation with the other students.

9) What was the order of the tasks they had to face?
   a. Flying keys, Fluffy, Snape's potions, Devil's Snare, Chess.
   b. Chess, Fluffy Snape's potions, Devil's Snare, Flying keys.
   c. Fluffy, Devil's Snare, Flying keys, Chess, Snape's potions.
   d. Fluffy, Devil's Snare, Flying keys, Snape's potions, Chess.

10) What surprised Harry about the final chamber?
   a. Snape was waiting for him.
   b. Dumbledore was already there.
   c. Voldemort was waiting.
   d. Neither Snape nor Voldemort were there.

___ / 10

Inferences

An *inference* is a conclusion you can make based on the information you are given. The answer is not directly given to you.

Answer the following questions by making inferences based on information from *Harry Potter and the Philosopher's Stone*. Circle **True** if the inference is correct, or **False** if the inference is incorrect. In one or two sentences, explain your answer.

1) Harry found it very easy to focus on school work.	TRUE	FALSE
Explanation:		

2) Ron was afraid he did poorly on his exams.	TRUE	FALSE
Explanation:		

3) Snape secretly hopes that Harry and his friends get into more trouble.	TRUE	FALSE

Explanation:

4) Teachers think Hermione is a very hard-working student.	TRUE	FALSE

Explanation:

5) Hermione is not very confident in her ability to solve puzzles.	TRUE	FALSE

Explanation:

_____ / 10

Vocabulary

Look up the meaning of the following words:

Sweltering	
Fret	
Frantically	
Caution	
Exasperation	

Create two sentences, using a different vocabulary word from the list above in each sentence.

Vocabulary Word: _____

Sentence:

Vocabulary Word: _____

Sentence:

_____ / 7

Chapter 17
The Man with Two Faces — Title Page

Chapter 17
The Man with Two Faces

Main Idea

In your own words, write a paragraph describing the main idea of *Chapter 17*. Use complete sentences in your answer. Remember, when describing the Main Idea of a story, you want to stick to the important pieces of information!

___ / 3

Recalling Facts

1) Who did Harry find in the last room beneath the school?
    a. Professor Snape.
    b. Professor Quirrell.
    c. Professor Dumbledore.
    d. Voldemort.

2) What was Harry shocked to discover?
    a. Quirrell was working with Snape.
    b. Snape was fighting with Quirrell for the Philosopher's Stone.
    c. Snape was trying to save Harry during Quidditch.
    d. Quirrell was trying to save Harry during Quidditch.

3) What is Professor Quirrell skilled with?
    a. Transfiguration.
    b. Seeing the future.
    c. Warding off vampires.
    d. Working with trolls.

4) What lie does Harry tell Professor Quirrell about what he sees in the Mirror of Erised?
    a. He is standing over a defeated Voldemort.
    b. He has won the House Cup.
    c. He has the Philosopher's Stone in his pocket.
    d. The students were all in danger.

5) Why does Voldemort want the Philosopher's Stone?
    a. To create the Elixir of Life.
    b. To turn objects into gold and gain unlimited wealth.
    c. To help kill Harry Potter.
    d. To stop the curse from drinking unicorn blood.

6) How did Harry defeat Voldemort and Quirrell?
- a. Harry didn't; he held on long enough for Dumbledore to help.
- b. Harry was blessed with his mother's love.
- c. Harry used the Philosopher's Stone against Voldemort.
- d. Quirrell couldn't touch Harry without getting burned.

7) What will happen now that the Philosopher's Stone has been destroyed?
- a. Voldemort can never return.
- b. Nicholas Flamel will die.
- c. Only Dumbledore will live forever.
- d. A new one will be created.

8) What allowed Gryffindor to finally defeat Slytherin for the House Cup?
- a. Ron winning the best game of chess Hogwarts has seen.
- b. Harry winning the final Quidditch game.
- c. Harry stopping Voldemort.
- d. Neville standing up to his friends.

9) What did the Weasley twins hope they wouldn't get?
- a. Warning notes to be better behaved the next year.
- b. A failing mark on their exams.
- c. Letters reminding them not to use magic over the summer.
- d. A lecture from their mother about toilet seats.

10) What makes Harry happier about spending another summer with the Dursleys?
- a. Dumbledore sent them a message to treat him better.
- b. The Dursleys have become kinder while he was at Hogwarts.
- c. They don't know he isn't allowed to use magic.
- d. He thinks he and Dudley may become friends.

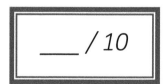

_____ / 10

Inferences

An ***inference*** is a conclusion you can make based on the information you are given. The answer is not directly given to you.

Answer the following questions by making inferences based on information from *Harry Potter and the Philosopher's Stone*. Circle **True** if the inference is correct, or **False** if the inference is incorrect. In one or two sentences, explain your answer.

1) Professor Quirrell has had previous experience with the Mirror of Erised.	TRUE	FALSE
Explanation:		

2) Voldemort values the lives of his followers.	TRUE	FALSE
Explanation:		

3) Professor Dumbledore was upset that Harry had found out about Nicholas Flamel.	TRUE	FALSE

Explanation:

_____

_____

_____

_____

4) Harry thought he was going to do poorly on his exams.	TRUE	FALSE

Explanation:

_____

_____

_____

_____

_____

5) Harry is going to use magic on Dudley over the summer.	TRUE	FALSE

Explanation:

_____

_____

_____

_____

_____

___ / 10

Vocabulary

Look up the meaning of the following words:

Stutter	
Displeased	
Petrified	
Tokens	
Bravery	

Create two sentences, using a different vocabulary word from the list above in each sentence.

Vocabulary Word: _____

Sentence:

Vocabulary Word: _____

Sentence:

___ / 7

Harry Potter and The Philosopher's Stone Bonus Activities

Novel Study Activity

Throughout this novel, you will meet many new and interesting characters! As a fun project, create popsicles stick puppets for each new character you meet!

For an added challenge, update your main character puppets as you work your way through this adventure! Change their clothing and look to match the book!

For a bonus activity, create an entire collection of Harry Popsicle characters and use them to create your own "Harry Popsicle" movie or booklet!

Name: _____

Chapter Activity

Based on the descriptions given in the chapter, draw a picture of one of the following characters: *Albus Dumbledore, Professor McGonagall, Hagrid, Vernon Dursley, Petunia Dursley*

©J.W. Crawford 2021. The classroom teacher may reproduce copies of materials in this book for classroom use only.

Chapter Activity

Based on the description in the chapter, draw a picture of what you think Harry's cupboard under the stairs would look like.

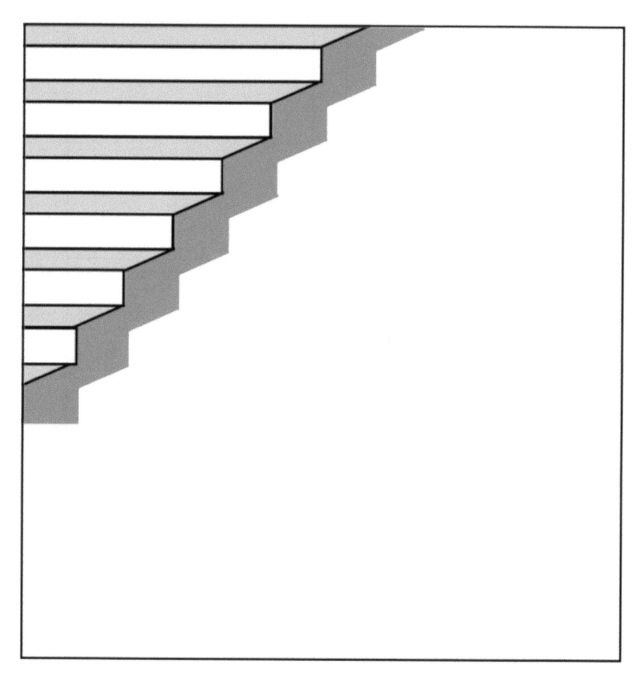

Name: _____

Chapter Activity

Create a 6-panel comic strip to illustrate one of the scenes from "Harry Potter and the Philosopher's Stone."

Chapter Activity

Colour the brick wall on the next page. After the wall is coloured, careful cut the wall down the middle to make a doorway into Diagon Alley.

Glue this page over top of your "Diagon Alley" illustration. Be careful to only glue around the edges. Leave the Brick wall doorway open, to give new wizards a peek into Diagon Alley!

1) Draw your "Diagon Alley" illustration, based on the description in the book. 	2) Colour your brick wall. 
3) Careful cut a doorway into your brick wall. 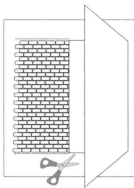	4) Glue the open doorway over your Diagon Alley illustration. 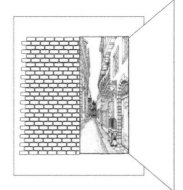

Draw a picture of Diagon Alley in the box below, using the description from Chapter 5! Make sure to colour your picture!

cut here   cut here

cut here   cut here

©J.W. Crawford 2021. The classroom teacher may reproduce copies of materials in this book for classroom use only.

Chapter Activity

Based on the description of Platform 9 ¾ in the chapter, draw a picture to show what you think the Hogwarts Express platform would look like when you walked through the barrier.

Chapter Activity

Examine the sorting hat descriptions for each house group in chapter 7. Write a brief paragraph on this robe. What house group do you think you would be chosen for? Explain why!

Afterwards, glue your house group robe on top! Be careful to only glue the edges and cut your house group robe in the middle so it opens up to read your thoughts!

Colour your ***Gryffindor*** robe, using the house group colours! When you are finished, cut your robe out, and cut along the middle line as well. You will be gluing these pieces onto the blank robe!

Colour your *Ravenclaw* robe, using the house group colours! When you are finished, cut your robe out, and cut along the middle line as well. You will be gluing these pieces onto the blank robe!

Colour your **Slytherin** robe, using the house group colours! When you are finished, cut your robe out, and cut along the middle line as well. You will be gluing these pieces onto the blank robe!

Colour your *Hufflepuff* robe, using the house group colours! When you are finished, cut your robe out, and cut along the middle line as well. You will be gluing these pieces onto the blank robe!

Chapter Activity

Draw what you would see reflected back at you from the Mirror of Erised! On the next page, explain why you would see that image.

Erised stra ehru oyt ube cafru oyt on wohsi

If you looked into the *Mirror of Erised*, what would you see? Write a paragraph explaining your reflection. Your paragraph should be between 4-5 sentences long and include why you would see that image. Start your paragraph with ***"If I looked into the Mirror of Erised, I would see . . ."***

Can you translate what the phrase carved into the Mirror of Erised says?
(Hint: How does a mirror work?)

Erised stra ehru oyt ube cafru oyt on wohsi

Chapter Activity

Yikes! You've gotten lost in the Forbidden Forest! Find your way through the forest and safely back to Hagrid's hut, without running into a werewolf!

Chapter Activity

Using the potions riddle from Harry Potter and the Philosopher's Stone, see if you can figure out which bottle would successfully help Harry move on to the next challenge! Place an 'X' in the boxes that wouldn't match the bottle, and a checkmark in the boxes that match the bottle. Circle the bottle on the table that you would drink from!

	1	2	3	4	5	6	7
Go through							
Go Back							
Poison							
Poison							
Poison							
Nettle Wine							
Nettle Wine							

Chapter Activity

Using a small or medium sized paper bag, create your own Professor Quirrell / Voldemort puppet!

On one side of the paper bag, design a nervous face to represent Professor Quirrell, using construction paper, coloured markers or pencils, or other art supplies of your choosing!

Flip the paper bag around.
On the reverse side, design a face that matches the description of Voldemort from the novel.

Using ribbon or light fabric or paper, create a removable turban that wraps around Quirrell's head and covers Voldemort's face!

Chapter Activity

Gryffindor wins the House Cup! Draw an illustration of the Great Hall, displaying the Gryffindor colours that now adorn the hall!

Alternate Activity: Draw an image of Professor Quirrell and Voldemort as they are described together.

Harry Potter and The Philosopher's Stone Final Project

Artistic	Artistic	Artistic
Create a Shoe Box diorama representing a scene from the novel.	Create a sculpture representing a scene from the novel.	Design a Wanted poster for one of the characters from the novel.
Artistic	**Narrative**	**Expository**
Create a scrapbook from the point of view of one of the students from Hogwarts.	Create a story from the point of view of one of the other characters in the novel, creating a Hogwarts adventure that happens while the main story is happening.	Create a pamphlet inviting tourists to Hogwarts.
Expository	**Expository**	**Expository**
Create a Television News Report about one of the events that happened at Hogwarts during the course of the novel.	Write a newspaper article reporting information about an event that happened at Hogwarts.	Create a Radio News Report based on an event that happened within the novel.

Project Explanations

For your final project based on our novel study for the novel, Harry Potter and the Philosopher's Stone, you will be completing three projects from a Tic-Tac-Toe board.

On this board, you will notice the middle box is shaded in. That is because this is a project that all students will be expected to complete. Where you go with the other two is partially up to you!

Every student will be responsible for *3* different projects. These will include:

a) Artistic
b) Narrative Writing Piece
c) Expository Information Piece

To pick your three choices, you will need to look at the board as you would a tic-tac-toe board. Each piece is selected according to each other, with the middle selection always being chosen.

For example: If you pick box 1, you must complete box 5 and box 9 with it. Here is the list of how the boxes go together.

1-5-9

2-5-8

3-5-7

4-5-6

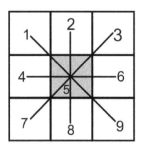

©J.W. Crawford 2021. The classroom teacher may reproduce copies of materials in this book for classroom use only.

Artistic:

With this portion of your final project, you will be completing one out of a possible four art choices.

1) **Shoe Box Diorama** – For this project, you will need to use a shoebox (or similar small box) to create a diorama representing a scene from the novel. Your diorama should be fairly detailed, including both characters and scenery from the scene, and should use several different types of materials (clay, paper, cardboard, Popsicle sticks, etc.)

2) **Sculpture** – Using clay, create a sculpture based on one of the scenes from the novel. Include other materials as you see fit! Your sculpture should have more than just one character.

3) **Wanted Poster** – Design a Wanted Poster for one of the characters from the novel. It does not necessarily have to be an antagonist, but your poster should include the reasons why they are wanted. It should include some vital information such as physical description, place last seen, etc.

4) **Scrapbook** – Create a scrapbook for a character from the novel, or from yourself as though you had attended Hogwarts. It should include several things, like photographs (or drawings), assignment marks, etc.

Narrative Writing Piece:

This portion of the project is assigned to everyone.

For this project, you are to write a creative story telling about an adventure from one of the other students in the class. If possible, try to have it be an adventure that takes place within Hogwarts while Harry is there for the first year.

For example:
When Harry and Ron first go to meet Draco Malfoy for a Wizard's Duel, they find Neville asleep outside the Gryffindor dormitory. What happened while Neville was locked out of the dorms?

For this project, you will be expected to complete and turn in both your planning page and your story. You can complete the story typed up or hand-written.

BONUS CONTEST!!!

If you feel like challenging yourselves, turn your story into a small movie! Write out a small script for your story, and create a film for it!

This will be a contest! All of the videos completed will be submitted to a contest, where a panel of judges will be chosen to watch the videos and vote for their favorite! The winning group will receive an award decided on by the class!

Expository Piece:

For this portion of your project, you will be asked to complete one of four possible expository choices. An expository work is one that gives information about a topic, rather than simply telling a story. For each of these, you will be expected to provide a list of what pages you found the information from for your piece. This will be your reference page.

For the Expository Project, feel free to enlist the help of your classmates!

a) ***Pamphlet*** – Create a pamphlet for tourists and visitors that will encourage them to come and visit Hogwarts School of Witchcraft and Wizardry, based on information found in the novel. You will want to include photos to make it look inviting, as well as a good deal of information from the book that will help explain why Hogwarts is a great place to visit.

b) ***Newspaper Article*** – Write a newspaper article reporting an event that took place at Hogwarts. Your article should include a Headline, Byline, and an informative article, including statements from witnesses to the event.

c) ***News Report*** – Create a News Report video reporting about an event that took place in the novel. You should try your best to make the report look professional and include at least one statement from a witness to the event as an interview.

d) ***News Radio Report*** – This is the same idea as the News Video, except that this will only be recorded using your voice.

Harry Potter
and the Philosopher's Stone

Novel Study Answer Key

The following pages contain the answer key for this novel study unit. For some of the questions, like the Main Idea and the Inferences, while answers are given, teachers and instructors will want to also use their own opinions and ideas to assess student work.

Chapter 1
The Boy Who Lived

Main Idea
Harry Potter was just a baby when he was attacked by Voldemort. Somehow, he survived, and Voldemort lost his power. Dumbledore has decided that the best place for Harry to grow up will be with his aunt and uncle, the Dursley's. This will help him grow up as normal as possible.

Recall Facts
1. d	2. a	3. b	4. a	5. c
6. d	7. b	8. a	9. d	10. a

Inferences

1.   *False*. Vernon Dursley feels uncomfortable around anything or anyone strange. The people he runs into makes him feel uneasy.

2.   *True*. Petunia Dursley loves being nosy. She tells Vernon all about Mrs. Next Door's problems.

3.   *True*. Dumbledore is very patient with Professor McGonagall, and with Hagrid when he is late.

4.   *False*. Hagrid cries when he thinks of Lilly and James Potter, and when he says goodbye to Harry.

5.   *True*. According to Dumbledore, living with the Dursleys will help keep Harry normal, and away from attention he is not ready for.

Vocabulary
Mysterious - of obscure nature, meaning, origin, etc.; puzzling; inexplicable.
Nonsense – words, language or conduct that is senseless or foolish.
Unusual – not common or ordinary.
Persuade – to convince somebody to do something.
Slinking – to move in a slow, careful way.

Chapter 2
The Vanishing Glass

Main Idea
Strange things happen to Harry Potter when he is stressed or upset. When Aunt Petunia cut his hair, it grew back by the next day. When he was being chased by bullies, he ended up on the school roof. At the zoo, when Dudley hits him, the glass in front of a snake tank disappears, letting the snake go free.

Recall Facts
1. a   2. a   3. c   4. c   5. d
6. c   7. d   8. c   9. a   10. b

Inferences
1.   *True*. Harry's dream mirrors what happened when he was a baby, when Hagrid delivered him to Dumbledore.

2.   *False*. Harry can't stand listening to stories about Mrs. Figg's cats and is excited to go to the zoo.

3.   *False*. The Dursleys worry he will ruin their house and car.

4.   *False*. When Piers says Harry was talking to the snake, Vernon locks him in his cupboard as punishment.

5.   *False*. Strange things keep happening to Harry, like his hair growing back, ending up on the school roof, etc.

Vocabulary
Mantelpiece – a shelf above a fireplace.
Cupboard - a closet with shelves for dishes, cups, etc.
Tantrum – a childish fit of rage or bad temper.
Jumper – a pullover sweater.
Gibber – to speak foolishly or meaninglessly.

Chapter 3
The Letters from No One

Main Idea

After the incident at the zoo, Harry is starting to realize there is something different about him. At home, a letter arrives, addressed to Harry in his cupboard under the stairs. Uncle Vernon won't let him have the letter. Soon, many more letters try to find him in various strange ways. Refusing to let Harry have the letters, Uncle Vernon tries to escape with his family to a small shack on a rocky island. As Harry tries to sleep, he remembers it's his birthday. All he wants is his letter.

Recall Facts

1. a	2. c	3. d	4. a	5. d
6. b	7. c	8. a	9. c	10. a

Inferences

1.   *True*. Dudley broke his new cine-camera, crashed his remote-control aeroplane and knocked down Mrs. Figg.

2.   *True*. Harry was looking forward to September, because he would finally be away from Dudley at school.

3.   *False*. Aunt Petunia was dying Dudley's old clothes grey, and they looked like old elephant skin.

4.   *True*. Harry had never gotten mail before. The letter was the first thing he had ever gotten.

5.   *False*. Uncle Vernon rented an old, rickety boat to get them across to the shack.

Vocabulary

Comprehensive – covering or involving much information.
Knickerbockers – short trousers gathered in at the knees.
Informed – having or prepared with information or knowledge.
Bawling – to cry or wail loudly.
Rations – an allotted amount; provisions.

Chapter 4
The Keeper of the Keys

Main Idea

Harry is shocked when a giant appears and informs Harry that he is a wizard. Harry learns that his parents weren't killed in a car crash, but instead were murdered by Voldemort. He also discovers that he is supposed to attend Hogwarts School of Witchcraft and Wizardry, starting in September.

Recall Facts

1. a	2. d	3. b	4. c	5. c
6. c	7. a	8. c	9. a	10. b

Inferences

1. *True*. When he enters the cabin, Hagrid knocks the door off its hinges. He easily lifts it back into place. He also ties Uncle Vernon's rifle into a knot.

2. *False*. Whenever Hagrid gets upset with him, Vernon quiets down very quickly and shies away.

3. *True*. She calls her sister *abnormal*.

4. *True*. He gets very upset when Dumbledore is insulted and stands up for him.

5. *True*. Dumbledore sent Hagrid to collect Harry, and to also stay on as gamekeeper after being expelled.

Vocabulary

Strode – walked with long steps, often arrogant.
Bewildered – completely puzzled or confused.
Quill – a feather formed into a pen for writing.
Scandal – a disgraceful action.
Expelled – to drive or force out of something.

Chapter 5
Diagon Alley

Main Idea
Hagrid takes Harry to Diagon Alley, where he gets to pick up his school supplies. While there, Harry realizes that he is very well known. He also realizes he doesn't know much about the wizarding world. At Gringotts, the wizards bank, Harry discovers that his parents left him a lot of money. Hagrid also has an important item to pick up from the bank.

Recall Facts

1. c	2. a	3. d	4. a	5. c
6. b	7. a	8. a	9. a	10. a

Inferences

1.   *True*. At the beginning of the chapter, he is very sad when he thinks it was all a dream. When he gets to Diagon Alley, he is astonished by all of the magical stores.

2.   *False*. Hagrid mentions that the Ministry of Magic is messing things up, as usual.

3.   *True*. Quirrell seems very shy, and stutters while talking. A result of an encounter with vampires and a hag.

4.   *False*. When he meets people in the Leaky Cauldron, he is surprised at how excited they are to meet him, and how many know who he is already.

5.   *True*. Hagrid takes his job very seriously and is incredibly proud that Dumbledore trusts him. He feels important because Dumbledore gave him a special task.

Vocabulary
Cauldron – a large kettle or boiler.
Parchment – a type of material used to write on.
Awkwardly – lacking skill or grace.
Flitting – to move lightly and swiftly.
Destined – something that is predetermined to happen, or planned.

Chapter 6
The Journey from Platform Nine and Three-Quarters

Main Idea

Harry makes his way to King's Cross station, where, with the help of a wizard family, he makes it onto the Hogwarts Express. During the trip to Hogwarts, Harry meets a new friend named Ron Weasley. The two of them form a bond as they travel, becoming friends. When they finally arrive at Hogwarts, Harry realizes it is a very big castle.

Recall Facts

1. a	2. c	3. d	4. a	5. a
6. c	7. d	8. b	9. c	10. c

Inferences

1. *False*. Uncle Vernon, thinking Harry won't be able to get on the train, leaves him alone at the station with no help.

2. *True*. Mrs. Weasley has several older children, and they know how to get to the platform because they have gone on the train before.

3. *False*. Harry is recognized by his scar, and students begin talking about him as soon as they realize who he is.

4. *True*. Draco insults Ron, calling his family poor.

5. *True*. Neville loses his toad, Trevor, while on the train to Hogwarts.

Vocabulary

Punctures – piercing a hole through something.
Platform – a raised, horizontal surface or structure.
Barrier – something natural or built that stops passage to another area.
Gawped – to stare in astonishment with the mouth open.
Compartment – a separate room or section

Chapter 7
The Sorting Hat

Main Idea
Now at Hogwarts, Harry and the other first year students are sorted into their houses. Each student is placed in one of four houses: Gryffindor, Ravenclaw, Hufflepuff or Slytherin. Harry learns that they will receive or lose points throughout the year, and the house with the most points at the end of the year will win the House Cup. The students also receive a warning about some dangers at Hogwarts that they need to be careful to avoid.

Recall Facts
1. c	2. a	3. c	4. d	5. a
6. a	7. c	8. b	9. a	10. c

Inferences
1. **False**. Professor McGonagall is a stern witch that gives the impression she shouldn't be crossed.

2. **False**. When the ghosts first arrive, Harry jumps, and many of the students scream in surprise.

3. **False**. Although we don't hear about anyone else, Harry manages to talk to the hat and convince that he shouldn't be in Slytherin.

4. **True**. Dumbledore has all the students sing a song, and afterwards says music is a magic beyond what they do at Hogwarts.

5. **True**. Peeves carried a bunch of walking sticks and dropped them on a student's head.

Vocabulary
Magnificent – extraordinarily fine.
Transparent – easily seen through, recognized, or detected.
Bewitched – to enchant, charm, fascinate.
Airily – in a lively or breezy manner; jauntily.
Dormitory – a building or room containing a number of beds; a sleeping quarter.

Chapter 8
The Potions Master

Main Idea
Harry begins getting to know his way around Hogwarts. He has his first class with Professor Snape, the head of Slytherin. Snape is a cold, almost cruel teacher, who seems to already dislike Harry. Harry also learns that Gringott's bank suffered a break in, but the vault, the same one he had visited with Hagrid earlier in the story, was empty and nothing was stolen.

Recall Facts
1. b	2. d	3. a	4. a	5. b
6. b	7. a	8. a	9. c	10. b

Inferences

1.   *True*. As he walks around Hogwarts, Harry hears many kids whispering about him.

2.   *False*. Filch uses his cat so he can try and catch students breaking rules and get them in trouble.

3.   *False*. The students thought they would enjoy it, but they find Professor Quirrell strange and don't learn about anything fun like they expected.

4.   *True*. Hermione has already studied her books and tries to answer many questions in class.

5.   *True*. Hagrid won't meet Harry's eyes when Harry asks about the break-in. He also quickly changes the subject.

Vocabulary
Queuing – a file or line; waiting for a turn.
Subtle – fine or delicate in meaning or intent.
Register – a list of records, events, names, etc.
Investigations – searching for facts.
Grubby – dirty, slovenly

Chapter 9
The Midnight Duel

Main Idea

Harry has his first flying lesson, and discovers he is a natural on the broom. He is so good, in fact, that he gets invited to join the Gryffindor Quidditch team. After a confrontation with Malfoy during the lesson, Harry is challenged to a midnight duel, which he and Ron accept. It is a trick, though, and instead of fighting Malfoy, they end up meeting a giant, three-headed dog that seems to be guarding something.

Recall Facts

1. a	2. d	3. b	4. c	5. a
6. a	7. d	8. a	9. a	10. d

Inferences

1.   *True*. Malfoy brags about his flying skill and is quick to jump on his broom as soon as Madam Hooch isn't around.

2.   *True*. Dean Thomas is a fan of soccer (football) and has a poster that doesn't move on his wall.

3.   *True*. While it told him he had forgotten something, he couldn't remember what he had forgotten.

4.   *True*. When Harry gets on his broom to chase Malfoy, he finds he is very good at flying; he is good enough to be invited to the Gryffindor Quidditch team.

5.   *False*. When Filch tries to get Peeves to help, Peeves taunts him and flies off, leaving Filch even more frustrated.

Vocabulary

Reasonably – agreeable to reason; sound judgment.
Boastful – bragging, arrogance.
Gloatingly – to look at or think about with great or excessive, often smug with satisfaction.
Quaver – to shake tremulously; quiver or tremble.
Puzzlement – being perplexed; confused.

Chapter 10
Hallowe'en

Main Idea

At the Hogwarts Hallowe'en feast, a troll is discovered wandering inside the castle. Students are told to go back to the dormitories, but Harry and Ron decide to go looking for Hermione, who has run away. They find both her and the troll in the girls' bathroom. Working together, they defeat the troll. Hermione is welcomed in as a friend.

Recall Facts

1. b	2. c	3. d	4. a	5. c
6. d	7. a	8. b	9. a	10. c

Inferences

1.   *False*. Hermione is upset that Harry broke the rules yet received a fantastic reward.

2.   *False*. The Seeker is the most important position, because they try to catch the Golden Snitch, earn 150 points, and end the game.

3.   *True*. After Charms class, Ron makes a rude comment about Hermione and says she has no friends.

4.   *False*. Professor McGonagall is shocked that they managed to beat it, and rewards Harry and Ron with house points for managing to do such a difficult task.

5.   *True*. Hermione demonstrates her loyalty by blaming herself for the troll encounter and keeping Harry and Ron from getting in trouble.

Vocabulary

Keen – showing a strong feeling or desire; eager.
Fluttered – to be tremulous or agitated; a state of nervous excitement.
Recited – to repeat the words of something, often from memory.
Substitutes – a person or thing serving in place of another.
Trousers – pants, usually loose fitting.

Chapter 11
Quidditch

Main Idea

Harry gets ready to play his first ever game of Quidditch. During the game, something goes wrong with his broom. It starts trying to throw him off. Hermione helps him by distracted Professor Snape, who she believes is cursing his broom. With her help, he manages to capture the Golden Snitch and win the game for Gryffindor.

Recall Facts

1. b	2. d	3. c	4. b	5. c
6. d	7. b	8. a	9. d	10. c

Inferences

1. **False**. Even though they tried to keep it a secret, news quickly spread that Harry had become the new Gryffindor Seeker.

2. **True**. Harry was so nervous he couldn't even bring himself to eat breakfast.

3. **True**. While calling the match, Lee Jordan often makes negative marks towards the Slytherin team.

4. **False**. When Hermione thinks Snape is cursing Harry, she quickly sets off to stop him. She lights his robes on fire to distract him.

5. **False**. Hagrid doesn't think a teacher at Hogwarts would try and steal whatever Fluffy was guarding.

Vocabulary

Foul – grossly offensive or dirty; unfair or unfavorable.
Restless – inability to remain at rest.
Chatter – talk rapidly in a foolish or purposeless way.
Revolting – disgusting; repulsive.
Jinx – something that is supposed to bring bad luck.

Chapter 12
The Mirror of Erised

Main Idea

Christmas has come, and Harry and Ron will be staying at Hogwarts for the holiday. During their break, the two boys are determined to discover more about Nicholas Flamel. As a present, Harry receives an invisibility cloak from an anonymous person. He uses it to get into the Restricted Section of the library. When he almost gets caught, Harry discovers a room holding a magical mirror, which shows him his heart's greatest desire.

Recall Facts

1. a	2. c	3. c	4. c	5. c
6. d	7. d	8. a	9. b	10. a

Inferences

1.   *False*. Ron was staying as well, and Harry was looking forward to Christmas without the Dursleys.

2.   *True*. Hagrid seems very defensive when the students ask about Nicholas Flamel and tells them to drop it.

3.   *True*. Madam Pince needs a signed note from a teacher, and only lets older students into the Restricted Section.

4.   *False*. Hermione's parents are Muggle dentists and wouldn't know about anyone from the wizarding world.

5.   *True*. The cloak had once belonged to his father, and it helped him feel a bit closer to his dad.

Vocabulary

Bucking – to throw or attempt to throw; kicking motion to dislodge.
Blossoming – to flourish; develop.
Restricted – limited to or admitting only members of a particular group.
Feeble – weak, physically, intellectually, or morally; lacking.
Luminous – lighted up or illuminated; enlightened.

Chapter 13
Nicholas Flamel

Main Idea

After Dumbledore convinces Harry to leave the Mirror of Erised alone, Harry starts to focus more heavily on Quidditch. He learns that Professor Snape is going to be referring the next match. Before the match, Harry realized he has heard of Nicholas Flamel before, on the back of a chocolate frog wizard card. After winning their Quidditch match, Harry follows Professor Snape into the Forbidden Forest, where he overhears Snape threatening Professor Quirrell. This leads Harry to believe that Quirrell is protecting the Philosopher's Stone.

Recall Facts

1. c	2. a	3. d	4. b	5. b
6. b	7. d	8. a	9. b	10. a

Inferences

1.   *False*. Professor Snape is the head of Slytherin house, Gryffindor's rivals, and doesn't like Gryffindor. This will make him biased against the Gryffindor team.

2.   *True*. Hermione is good at everything. Having something to challenge her will be good to keep her from getting too arrogant.

3.   *False*. Jordan gets bored easily and wants to be in a world like the ones he draws.

4.   *True*. During the game, Ron finally snaps and attacks Malfoy, getting into a fist fight with him.

5.   *True*. Professor Quirrell always seems very afraid and nervous and wouldn't be confident enough to stop someone from getting the stone.

Vocabulary

Roaming – to walk, go, or travel without a fixed purpose.
Curse – a formula or charm intended to cause misfortune on another.
Alchemy – a form of chemistry; mixing of ingredients, often medicinal.
Steadied – firmly fixed; stable position.
Alarm – a sudden fear or distressing suspense; associated often with danger.

Chapter 14
Norbert the Norwegian Ridgeback

Main Idea
Harry, Ron and Hermione visit Hagrid to get more information on the Philosopher's Stone. While there, they discover that Hagrid has a dragon egg. The egg hatches, and Hagrid begins to raise a Norwegian Ridgeback. During a visit, Draco Malfoy spies on them through a window in Hagrid's hut. He goes to tell on the students and gets in trouble himself. Wanting to help Hagrid move Norbert, the dragon, before he gets in trouble, they help send the dragon to Charlie, Ron's brother who works with Dragons. After the dragon departs, they are caught out of bed by Filch, the Hogwarts caretaker.

Recall Facts

1. d	2. a	3. a	4. c	5. d
6. b	7. b	8. c	9. d	10. b

Inferences
1. *True*. Ron tells off other students that are making fun of Quirrell's stutter.

2. *True*. Hagrid thinks they are still trying to find information on Nicholas Flamel, even after he told them not to.

3. *False*. The Ministry of Magic works hard to put spells on Muggles who see dragons so that they forget about what they saw.

4. *False*. It's illegal for wizards to own dragons. It was turned into a law in 1709.

5. *True*. When she is scolding Malfoy, Professor McGonagall is wearing a nightgown and hairnet.

Vocabulary
Revision – the process of revising (editing) something or studying something.
Longingly – strong, persistent desire or craving.
Philosopher – a person who offers views or profound theories; alchemist.
Flattering – to try and please by complimentary remarks or attention.
Handkerchief – piece of fabric used to wipe one's nose and face.

Chapter 15
The Forbidden Forest

Main Idea

As part of his punishment for being caught out of bed, Harry has to serve detention by helping Hagrid with some chores in the Forbidden Forest. Something has been hurting unicorns, and Hagrid needs to find out what. Along with Harry, Malfoy, Neville and Hermione are also helping Hagrid. During the search, Harry sees a villainous creature drinking unicorn blood. The creature spots Harry, but luckily a group of centaurs arrive and save him. Harry learns that the creature from the forest may have been Voldemort.

Recall Facts

1. d	2. a	3. b	4. c	5. d
6. a	7. a	8. c	9. a	10. b

Inferences

1. *False*. Harry noticed that Neville looked incredibly hurt and felt like he had been tricked by Harry and his friends.

2. *True*. The Gryffindor team wouldn't speak to him, and would only call him "the Seeker," instead of using his name.

3. *False*. Malfoy's voice was panicked, and he tried to use his father as a threat so he wouldn't have to go in. He was also afraid of werewolves.

4. *True*. The centaurs look up at the stars often and talk about Mars repeatedly.

5. *False*. Voldemort was afraid of only one other wizard, Dumbledore. Dumbledore is thought to be the most powerful wizard.

Vocabulary

Astronomy – the science that deals with the universe beyond Earth's atmosphere.
Ashamed – feeling shame; embarrassed.
Rebellion – resistance to or defiance of authority.
Towering – very high or tall.
Undergrowth – low-lying vegetation or small trees.

Chapter 16
Through the Trapdoor

Main Idea
After realizing that Professor Snape was going to try and steal the Philosopher's Stone, and that Dumbledore wasn't around, Harry, Ron and Hermione decide they need to stop Snape themselves. To do this, they have to get past the protective challenges that were set to guard the stone. As they battle through, finally Harry is able to get to the final challenge, where he comes face to face with the thief, and realized that it isn't Professor Snape at all.

Recall Facts
1. a	2. a	3. c	4. b	5. d
6. b	7. b	8. a	9. c	10. d

Inferences
1.   *False*. The story mentioned that over the years afterwards, Harry didn't know how he managed to get through all his school work with the problems he was thinking about.

2.   *True*. When Hermione tries to talk about the exams afterwards, Ron starts to feel ill.

3.   *True*. Snape threatens to get them expelled from Hogwarts if they cause more problems.

4.   *True*. Hermione performs so well on her exams that the teachers wouldn't dare have her kicked out of Hogwarts.

5.   *True*. When she realizes that Snape's potion challenge is a puzzle, she doesn't get nervous, but instead becomes very excited.

Vocabulary
Sweltering – suffering oppressive heat.
Fret – to feel or express worry, annoyance, etc.
Frantically – desperate or wild with excitement, passion, fear, pain, etc.
Caution – alertness and care; a warning against danger.
Exasperation – extreme annoyance or irritation.

Chapter 17
The Man with Two Faces

Main Idea

Quirrell is waiting for Harry, not Professor Snape. At the final challenge, Quirrell is trying to figure out how to get the Philosopher's Stone from the Mirror of Erised. Harry is shocked to realize that the mirror places the stone in his pocket. He finds out that Voldemort has actually attached himself to Quirrell, and has been using him to stay alive. Voldemort knows Harry has the stone, and forces Quirrell to attack. Harry manages to survive long enough for Quirrell to be stopped. After stopping Voldemort for a second time, Harry finished the school year and heads home for another summer with the Dursleys.

Recall Facts

1. b	2. c	3. d	4. b	5. a
6. a	7. b	8. d	9. c	10. c

Inferences

1.   *False*. Quirrell is trying to examine the mirror when Harry first arrives. He has no idea how it works.

2.   *False*. Voldemort can be cruel and harsh to Quirrell when he doesn't feel Quirrell has satisfied his demands.

3.   *False*. Dumbledore was very patient with Harry, and was delighted when Harry mentioned Flamel.

4.   *True*. Harry was very surprised to learn he had passed all his exams.

5.   *False*. Using magic isn't allowed, but he will pretend in order to tease Dudley.

Vocabulary

Stutter – faltering or interrupted; broken speech
Displeased – to incur dissatisfaction or disapproval.
Petrified – to paralyze with astonishment, horror, or strong emotions.
Tokens – a momento; souvenir; keepsake.
Bravery – to show fearlessness or boldness

Milton Keynes UK
Ingram Content Group UK Ltd.
UKHW051121241023
431235UK00012B/370